TODAY'S RAILWAYS
REVIEW
OF THE YEAR

VOLUME 1

HOWARD JOHNSTON
STEVEN KNIGHT

▲Many metropolitan authorities in the UK were preparing plans for LRT systems in 1987, but London actually got its Docklands scheme into operation. Officially opened by H.M. The Queen on 30th July, the system carried its first passengers on 31st August. Three days later, German-built car No. 08 arrives at Tower Gateway from Island Gardens. *Hugh Ballantyne*

▼A light railway of a different kind was opened in Grenoble, France where a brand new tramway system was introduced. The revolutionary design of car with an extremely low floor height in the centre shown here has attracted the attention of many British Cities which are preparing plans for LRT schemes with street running involved. *Colin Birks*

CONTENTS

Written by Howard Johnston and Steven Knight with additional contributions from Roger Butcher, Peter Fox, Brian Garvin and Paul Jackson.

Published by Platform 5 Publishing Ltd., Lydgate House, Lydgate Lane, Sheffield S10 5FH.

Printed by Netherwood Dalton & Co., Huddersfield, England & BPCC Graphics, Slack Lane, Derby, England.

ISBN 0 906579 83 X

Further copies of this book may be obtained from Platform 5 Publishing Ltd. at the address shown above. Please enclose 10% of purchase price (UK) or 20% (abroad) to cover postage and packing.

▼Fifty years of progress at Doncaster Works. Class A4 4–6–2 4498 *SIR NIGEL GRESLEY* celebrated its 50th birthday with a return visit to The Plant on 12th February, and posed with what will almost certainly be the last loco ever to be produced there, Class 58 No. 58050. The works went through dramatic change from April 1 with its return to BR ownership as a 'level 5' maintenance depot for locos and DMUs, as well as the network's parts centre. *Les Nixon.*

Welcome to Today's Railways – Review of the Year.

This book is intended to be a digest of the most important events of the year 1987 for British Rail, LRT & Metro systems and railway preservation, with a brief glance at the major happenings on the Continent. As this is our first edition, and it was not until early this year that we learnt that a book on a similar theme from another publisher was definitely not to be published again, the book has appeared somewhat later than would normally be desirable. However, we hope that readers will find it was worth waiting for, and we can promise much earlier publication next year.

For British Rail, the underlying theme was to get the business into a healthy enough position to cope with an ever-decreasing government subsidy. Even so, the re-payment of interest charges is a major worry – they, plus high bills for restructuring Freightliners and BREL, turned the 1986/87 operating profit of £73.7 million into an £82.6 million overall loss.

Presenting the 1986/87 accounts, BR chairman Sir Robert Reid spoke of the successes of current policy: BR is ahead of its target, set in 1983, to reduce Government support from £980 million to £736 million. BR achieved a profit of £2.4 million after payment of interest charges, the best for three years. The three passenger sectors all reduced their operating losses. Railfreight returned to profit, showing a recovery from the worst effects of the miners' strike.

These were the facts:

InterCity. Earnings increased by 3.5%, gross income £657.6 million, operating loss £99.4 million before interest. 77% of trains arrived on time compared with 73% the year before. Greater attention was given to on-train catering and carriage cleaning.

Provincial. Operating loss reduced to £473.6 million, thanks to 4% passenger growth and much-reduced working expenses.

Network SouthEast. Operating loss of £162.3 million, gross income £709.6 million. Traffic up 4.5%. The One Day Capitalcard was a massive success with sales at a million a month.

Railfreight. Operating surplus of £25 million on £556.6 million gross income. Highlights were creation of sub-sectors, increased crew productivity, new domestic coal network, and concentration of train ferries on Dover–Dunkerque route.

Parcels. Operating loss of £3 million of turnover of £118.9 million, but £9.1 net profit after interest rebates. There was success with Red Star and letter mail but problems with newspapers and magazines.

Freightliner. Operating loss of £6.4 million on gross income of £104.7 million. Many depots were closed, with attention turned to deep-sea traffic and long-haul traffic to Ireland, Western Europe and within the UK.

Travellers Fare. Record operating surplus of £5.5 million on turnover of £67.7 million. There was a move into more fast food.

BREL. Net loss of £5.3 million on turnover of £452.3 million. Massive restructuring is underway.

Behind the balance sheet, a host of new developments gave planners, railwaymen and travellers good cause for optimism, as the pages of this book will unfold.

The enthusiast had another good year with a host of big events both in preservation and on the mainline. This book would not have been possible without the help of some of Britain's finest photographers, and our sincere thanks go to them.

HOWARD JOHNSTON & STEVEN KNIGHT.
(Authors)

PETER FOX. (Publisher)

REVIEW OF THE YEAR 1988

Contributions for Volume Two will be most welcome. Good quality black and white photographs and colour transparencies (previously unpublished please) reflecting important events and developments should be securely packed and sent to the following address:

Today's Railway – Review of 1988,
Platform 5 Publishing Ltd,
Lydgate House,
Lydgate Lane,
Sheffield. S10 5FH.

Preparation of the next edition will start in mid-October 1988, and contributors should have submitted the bulk of their work by that date (other than important items which occur later in the year).

Title page: InterCity used its 21st birthday on 1st May to demonstrate what progress has been made in passenger comfort. 1966 was re-created with a special run from Euston to Liverpool with Class AL6 loco No. E 3195 (alias 86426, part-restored to original livery style) and a rake of maroon Mark 1 coaches. The formation is seen passing Halewood.
David Rapson.

◄ Forty years of progress on the Southern. On the left, the early post war concept of commuter travel is depicted in restored Class 405 4 Sub unit No. 4732, whose features in later slam-door 4 EPB units will be part of every-day life at least into the early 1990s. On the right, a new sliding-door Class 319 unit will capitalise on the reopening of the cross-London Snow Hill tunnel to provide a through "Thameslink" service from Bedford to North Kent and the South Coast from 1988. Both were displayed at Waterloo on 24th October.
Colin Marsden.

BRITAIN'S RAILWAYS IN 1987

THE POLITICAL SCENE

For Britain's railway system, the most important date on the railway calendar was without doubt 11th June, when the country's voters re-elected a Conservative government that is committed to big changes. However the government's view of the railways as a business brought its fair share of criticism from the large lobby of people who see the railways as primarily a service.

1987 will be remembered as the year of the Sector, when after much talking the individual parts of BR went their own distinct ways, with moves to greater profit by privatisation and attempts to slash inefficient operations such as British Rail Engineering Limited.

Whatever political party you supported, there was cause for a great deal of justified optimism from three major investment schemes – the Channel Tunnel, a variety of urban rapid transit systems, and new rolling stock for InterCity, Provincial and Network SouthEast. The Channel Tunnel was by far the biggest ray of sunshine as plans unfolded and work started towards the 1993 completion target. The promoters suffered as much as any other corporation with the October Stock Exchange shares collapse, although there was a major boost of enthusiasm when it was revealed that traffic projections were so vast that extra tunnels are already being contemplated. Will BR then be forced to build its high-speed line from London to Kent? Eleven firms, seven of them British, were invited on 19th May to submit tenders for the 40 units of 200 km/h BR/300 km/h SNCF rolling stock.

In Britain itself, 1987 saw several undertakings announce plans for high-tech light rapid transit systems. While London's lavish Docklands Railway was inaugurated on 31st August (a month late), Manchester demonstrated its determination to get public support by borrowing a Docklands unit to run on a piece of demonstration track. Not to be outdone, the West Midlands knocked the dust off its scheme, and in mid-November a Private Bill was deposited in Parliament for a £385 million Avon Metro LRT system.

Internally, BR had the first regional shake-up since the demise of the North Eastern Region in the mid-1960s with the announcement on 22nd September of a new Anglia Region to concentrate managerial resources in the country's fastest growing area without the need to resort to decisions from far-off York.

The year was not without its banana skins however. The Government's much-vaunted deregulation of the buses brought unexpected but welcome extra traffic for PTE-supported city urban rail networks, along with operating headaches because new rolling stock was simply unreliable.

Two major Scottish rail issues festered. The first was the Dornoch Rail Bridge. Although the Scottish Office confirmed that the project was dead because the £12 million cost outweighed social benefits, moles within the department suggested a strong bias towards the road lobby. The outcry was such that police were called in to discover where the embarrassing leak started. The second was the Faslane nuclear submarine depot. It was in 1986 that it was decided to spend a massive £10 million on a temporary road to aid construction work when rail improvements would have only cost a fraction of the cost. In the event, rail benefited anyway because some of the steel piling was too long for lochside roads.

The case for the closure of the scenic Settle and Carlisle line was also rocked at its foundations when it was revealed that Ribblehead Viaduct was not falling down quite as fast as had been made out, whilst the massive upturn in traffic suggested the route was actually paying its way. Across the Pennines, the city of Bradford was justifiably irked by the disconnection of the Wortley Curve, a short spur that ended any hope of a through service to London without going via Leeds. There was little traffic anyway, but BR should have gone through the statutory procedures before taking the action it did.

ROUTES

If 1987 lacked announcements of major new civil engineering projects, it was none the less exciting because it witnessed the completion of others which were authorised earlier. Without doubt the major showpiece was the inauguration of electric services from Ipswich to Norwich from May, although two other Eastern Region electric services were also worthy of headlines. Commuters to Huntingdon and Peterborough got the high-frequency service they had been denied since the wires stopped at Hitchin in 1976. They were far from happy however at losing their 125 m.p.h. HSTs for 100 m.p.h. Class 317 EMUs with inferior seating. The nearby Bishops Stortford–Cambridge electric service also came on stream, although on this occasion daily travellers were quick to rumble that their EMU stock was in fact older than the Mark 2 hauled stock it replaced.

On Clydeside, the £85 million Ayrshire scheme was formally completed with the introduction of electric services to Largs and Ardrossan Harbour on 19th January, with news that traffic at some stations had increased by 20 per cent.

Whilst electrification teams worked flat out on the massive £306 East Coast scheme and at the year end ceremonially strung up wires over the England–Scotland border, two minor infilling projects were given Government approval, the 13-mile Royston–Cambridge link, and 6-mile Watford–St. Albans branch.

Talking third rail electrification, the InterCity electric services Weymouth was denied when the investment was halted at Bournemouth in 1967 became closer reality, while in London the "Thameslink" via Snow Hill Tunnel was energised ready for the 1988 Bedford–Brighton through service.

Less dramatic, but nevertheless important, was the re-introduction of passenger services on three lines, Corby–Kettering, Oxford–Bicester, Coventry–Nuneaton, plus a completely new Cardiff City Line service. Station re-openings were again in some profusion, but none greater than the return to the BR timetable on 4th October of Snow Hill (Birmingham), and some minnows in the shape of Haddenham and Thame Parkway, and Lake on the Isle of Wight. Rotherham Central station was reopened on a site slightly to the east of the original station of the same name, some 14 years after this was first suggested by your publisher.

After minor prunings in recent years, the rest of the system's passenger route mileage stayed remarkably intact during 1987. The threatened Huddersfield–Penistone service was reprieved for the second time in seven years with a grant from West Yorkshire Passenger Transport Authority. Other suggested closures didn't happen either – the four-mile Warwickshire Henley-in-Arden and Bearley Junction link became the subject of a BR/local council compromise plan, and the tiny Rowntree Halt at York with its reputed three regular passengers became subject of an expensive public inquiry. The extensive MOD sidings complex at Bramley near Basingstoke closed on 1st March, but ironically carried its first BR-sponsored passenger train the same day!

An interesting project mooted during 1987 was to divert the Newquay line from Par to St. Austell by means of relaying a short length of track south of St. Dennis Junction, to enable closure of the troublesome St. Dennis–Bugle section of the current route, and establish a shorter route to the West of England Main Line. One change on the freight scene was somewhat dramatic. It was goodbye to the entire Severn Tunnel Junction marshalling yard at a stroke on October 10 after 151 busy years, to be replaced by smaller shunting yards at East Usk and Gloucester. Down the line at Margam, the still-modern but under-used yard was completely replaced on 1st November by a new 18-road Knuckle Yard to handle mostly local steel traffic.

Something that could not have possibly been planned for was the utter chaos of 16th October when severe overnight 100 m.p.h. storms swept across the southern half of England. A thousand miles of catenary on the Eastern Region was wrecked in 10 minutes, and power failures, thousands of fallen trees, landslips and chalk falls dislocated virtually the entire Southern Region. Dover's new Western Docks train ferry pier was destroyed, and a quarter of a mile of trees fell like dominoes at Sole Street. It took ten days to fully restore services. Barely had that damage been cleared up when the Shrewsbury–Llanelli route was severed by bridge collapse at Glanrhyd near Llandeilo on 19th October. Sadly, three passengers and a train driver died because a DMU went across it and plunged into the water below. BR has given a commitment to re-open the line.

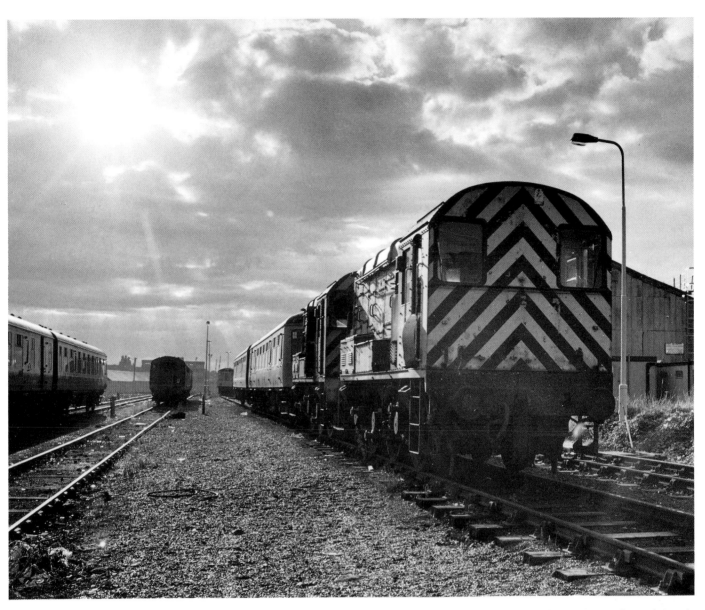

▲Sunset over Lincoln traction maintenance depot on 27th September which was one of many to be closed during 1987 as a direct victim of changed working practices associated with reduction of motive power and new builds of stock requiring less attention. Casualties on the Eastern Region included March, Lincoln, Hull Botanic Gardens, York Clifton, on the Southern, St Leonards (Hastings), and on the Western Severn Tunnel Junction. The picture shows Class 08 shunters Nos. 08242, 08386 and Class 114 DMUs.   *Brian Morrison.*

◄Construction work began in earnest on the Channel Tunnel during 1987, and this is the England end at Shakespeare Cliff near Folkestone as steelwork starts to arrive. On the left of this **4th** September picture, Class 411 unit No. 1566 is on a Margate–Charing Cross working.
                    Michael Collins.

►St. Blazey depot, one the few surviving roundhouses inherited from the steam age was displaced by new servicing facilities for the area's china clay locomotives and wagon fleet. Pleasingly, the buildings are protected from demolition, and have been sold for conversion. On 22nd April, Class 37 No. 37175 is on the depot turntable. Since then, the arrival of a replacement refurbished Class 37 fleet has seen this loco despatched to Inverness.
                    Les Nixon.

▲One of the more interesting projects to emerge was the scheme to divert the Newquay branch to Burngullow Junction by relaying two miles of track, allowing the troublesome six-mile section between Par and St Dennis Junction to be closed, and the expensive to maintain A30 girder bridge to be removed. At present, the Burngullow branch is used for china clay traffic as far as Parkandillack Works, and Class 47/3 No. 47314 heads a St Blazey-bound mixed freight near Lanjeth on 24th June.   *Geoff Gillham.*

◀In the North East, the Newcastle Riverside Branch on the north side of the Tyne was cut back from Wallsend to Shepherd's scrapyard at St Peter's, and there was prospect of it being eliminated completely to Riverside Junction on the ECML because of impending electrification. It remained double track to the end, and Class 31 No. 31271 is seen heading the trip freight from Tyne Yard to Shepherd's just before closure.   *Michael Rhodes.*

MAINTENANCE

A complete and radical restructuring of BR's maintenance and repair policy and practice took effect on 1st April. The reasons were threefold – the declining workload based on low-maintenance replacement rolling stock and subsequent reduction in older types; the continuing need to reduce overall costs; the new policy of open tendering for new build and some repair work.

The broad base of the plan was to create two new companies. British Rail Engineering Limited would retain facilities at Crewe, Derby Litchurch Lane, Derby Loco and York for new build, export, and heavy overhaul work on components such as power units and bogies.

At the same time, BREL sites would become candidates for privatisation in compliance with current Government thinking. (Doncaster's wagon works was the first to go this way before the year end. The rest, with the exception of Horwich foundry, would be sold as one concern).

Competitive tendering no longer guaranteed any new stock build, evident by the increased activity in DMU construction by Metro-Cammell of Birmingham and British Leyland at Workington.

A new company, British Rail Maintenance Limited, would absorb the former works at Doncaster, Eastleigh, Springburn (Glasgow), and Wolverton into a 14-strong chain of depots capable of heavy ("level five") stock maintenance. Other depots would gain "level" classifications to reflect their overall importance.

A key feature of the new plan was Component Exchange Overhaul, whereby stock could return to the rails much quicker if the stock arrived on depot at the same time as freshly overhauled components. Worn parts could be quickly replaced and overhauled at specially upgraded depots. The ultimate benefit would be a need for less locomotives and stock, at the same time more reliable because of dedication to particular duties.

The concentration of work on fewer more specialised depots would also enable economies at other depots, including closures. Doncaster would also become the major spare parts centre, known as Railpart, with a controversial road (not rail) distribution service. Not surprisingly, the effect on jobs at BREL was dramatic. March 17 saw the announcement that 1411 jobs had to go (Crewe 600, York 350, Derby Carriage 311, BREL HQ 100, Derby Loco 50). Far worse, the unions were told on September 22 that another 2970 had to go (Crewe 1050, Derby Carriage and Loco 1420, and York 500).

This was the defined workload:

BREL:

Crewe: New Class 90 and 91 assembly. Heavy classified repairs to Class 37; power units and bogies. Some contract work for BRML.

Derby Litchurch Lane: New builds of DMU, EMU and coaching stock when available, HST trailer and carriage conversion and overhaul.

Derby Loco: Class 08, 20 and HST power car overhauls (all to end March 1988). Locomotive bogies.

York: New builds of DMU and EMU. Maintenance of older coaching stock.

Level Five Depots:

Doncaster: Final few Class 31 refurbishments, repairs to Nottinghamshire and Yorkshire Class 56 and 58 freight locos, plus Classes 08, 20, 37, 47, and new-type Leeds, Manchester and Newcastle DMUs.

Stratford: Expanded to handle classified repairs to all a.c. electric locos, and LM, ER and WR diesels, power units and bogies, major repainting work.

Glasgow Springburn: Scottish Region locomotives, DMU, EMU and coaching stock, power unit and bogie repairs.

Eastleigh: SR loco work, DEMU and EMUs.

Wolverton: EMU refurbishment and repairs; coaching stock.

Leeds Neville Hill: ER and SCR HST power cars, ER first and second generation DMUs.

Ilford: GN and GE EMUs, coaching stock repairs and conversions.

Selhurst: Minor SR loco repairs, major DEMU and EMU work.

Slade Green: Major DEMU and EMU repairs, Shunter cab refurbishment.

Ashford Chart Leacon: DEMU, EMU repairs, bogie and electrical repairs.

Bristol Bath Road: West of England HST and DMU heavy repairs.

Plymouth Laira: Class 50s, South West DMUs.

Birkenhead North: Merseyrail Class 507 and 508 EMUs.

BREL Crewe (on contract from BR): LMR Class 37, 47, 56, 81, 85.

Other Depots are classified as follows:-
Level 1: Fuelling point only.
Level 2: A and B exams.
Level 3: All exams, with covered pits and light lifting facilities.
Level 4: As level three, but with larger staff and possibly cranes and heavy jacks for bogie removal, and possibly a wheel lathe.

▲Stratford DRS went through a massive transformation, and job recruitment programme as it was elevated to the status of London's major loco repair depot with 'level five' status. This photo dated 27th February shows the high standard of finish long associated with this former Great Eastern centre – the first Class 86 No. 86228 *Vulcan Heritage* sports the Stratford trademark of black front end marker light panels. On its right is Class 47 No. 47526. *Colin Marsden.*

▲Inside Stratford, Class 87 No. 87021 *Robert the Bruce* was also the first of its type to receive attention on the same day, 27th February. The loco is being stripped down prior to rebuilding, and will emerge within days in InterCity livery.   *Colin Marsden.*

▼All change at Springburn, where BREL ownership has given way to a new role as a BR 'level five CEM' depot. On 16th June, the project was given a musical send off when pipers heralded the naming of freshly overhauled Class 47/4 loco No. 47637 *Springburn*. The loco was later transferred to the Western Region!   *Tom Noble.*

SIGNALLING

EASTERN REGION:

Europe's longest single rail communications cable – from London to Edinburgh – was connected on 26th January, and to the chagrin of scrap metal enthusiasts is a high-tech, all plastic fibre optic affair with little recovery value. The £3.3 million project, with a loop for Wakefield and Leeds, is a vital part of the East Coast electrification project.

The end of the complex collection of diamond crossings at the north of Newcastle Central station was announced by the Eastern Region in a resignalling scheme that would cover 120 miles of East Coast Main Line between Northallerton and Berwick by 1990 with a new power box at Gateshead.

Attempts to improve the bottleneck approach to London's Liverpool Street station would be helped by a new scheme for nearby Bethnal Green.

LONDON MIDLAND REGION:

The third and final stage of the £22 million Leicester area resignalling scheme was completed on 6th December with the removal of the last semaphores between Wellingborough and Glendon Juction, Kettering, completing the 55-mile section between the edge of the West Hampstead (London) area and Trent (Notts) power box. At Kettering, the fourth running line was removed after the changeover to bi-directional working on the other three. Corby has been much simplified, and plans laid to single the line from Manton Junction and over Harringworth viaduct. The second stage between Leicester Humberstone Road to Loughborough had been completed during April.

▲A picture which requires little elaboration, except that it symbolises the completion of a missing link of the Midland Main Line resignalling scheme between Bedford and Market Harborough. Several of the boxes were bought for preservation. *Iain Scotchman.*

▼Never much in the headlines, even Hartlepool witnessed changes with the removal the imposing semaphore gantries protecting the station area in favour of colour lights. A DMU departs on 15th July. *Michael Rhodes.*

▲The new £3 million signalling and communications centre at Inverness was officially opened on 3rd June, featuring the first application in the UK of production solid state interlocking. It also spelled the end of five manually-controlled boxes, and will be fully operational with RETB installed over all long-distance lines by 1990. On 15th April, Class 47 No. 47448 stands outside the locomotive depot at the platform end. Also in view is the recently commissioned carriage maintenance depot. *Tom Noble.*

▼The Southern has implemented large numbers of piecemeal resignalling schemes, as well as the major project as part of the East Grinstead electrification. On the South Coast, the Portslade–Angmering project was well under way. On 29th May, renumbered Class 421 4 Cig unit No. 1266 arrives at Angmering with the 10.45 Littlehampton–Brighton. New colour light signals and close circuit cameras are in place awaiting commissioning. *Chris Wilson.*

SCOTTISH REGION:

Signalling around the Highland capital of Inverness can be regarded as a technological breakthrough because it represents the first production application in the UK of solid state interlocking. The fine arrays of semaphore signals, served by seven signalboxes dating back to Highland Railway days, were swept aside from 23rd June by a £3 million colour light system that followed many months of work that included severe pruning of irrelevant trackwork. Gone in favour of a power box are wooden cabins at Rose Street Junction, Millburn, the most famous Welsh's Bridge and the tiny Loco Cabin, and Culloden to the South.

Next in line for conversion was the manual missing link from Clachnaharry to Dingwall on the Far North Line, where RETB (Radio Electronic Token Block) comes into its own, and installation of RETB east of Nairn on the Aberdeen line, perhaps by 1990.

At Yoker, Glasgow, a new control centre was created to replace 17 manual boxes on 65 miles of the northern suburban system, this being largest solid state interlocking system on BR.

SOUTHERN REGION:

Linked to the Sanderstead–East Grinstead electrification scheme, a new power box was commissioned at Oxted on 11th July, incorporating the region's first solid state interlocking system.

A new Wimbledon control centre was constructed to handle the new signalling on the Leatherhead–Effingham Junction line.

WESTERN REGION:

The familiar sight of Great Western lower quadrant semaphores in the West of England main line is no more, following the completion in May 1987 of the £35 million scheme to inaugurate a new power box at Exeter, controlling 107 route miles from Athelney to Totnes.

The entire project, which also involved considerable track simplification, has eliminated 30 manual signalboxes, and 85 signalmen's jobs.

Faster line speeds will be possible under the new multiple aspect system, where bi-directional control has avoided the need for all but one diamond crossing (near Exeter St David's station), and termination of unfitted freights removed the need for 35 sets of catch points. Again, one has been kept between Exeter St David's and Central for safety reasons. Points are down from 557 to 294, and 20 miles of redundant running track removed.

The May 1987 timetable saw big changes in the West of England, not least a further stage in the resignalling scheme. 2nd May saw the abolition of Dainton Tunnel signalbox (pictured) and associated mechanical signalling to the new Exeter panel. Class 50s, such as No. 50028 *Tiger* on the 1030 Penzance–Liverpool on 28th April, lost their InterCity status. *Geoff Gillham.*

InterCity 21

As part of the celebrations of 21 years of Inter-City trains (or should it be 21 years of the words "Inter-City" to denote main express train services), BR laid on a special train from Euston to Liverpool hauled by E 3195 (86426). The coaching stock used was the 'Pullman Rail" Mark 1 FO set in maroon livery, although it should be remembered that the 1966 electric Euston–Manchester/Liverpool services were in fact mainly operated by blue and grey Mark 2s!

Stars of the 60s era such as the Searchers, Gerry Marsden and Dave Berry were present, plus DJ Mike Reid, who confesses to being a steam enthusiast. After a "rave-up" at Lime Street Station, a cruise down the Mersey was organised, with the Radio 1 'Gary Davis Show' being broadcast from the boat, the audience being a strange mixture of young people who had won a Radio 1 competition and railway and national journalists, mostly from the 50s and 60s era!

▶"Is it true that you collect Beanos Mike?"
Peter Fox

◀ Inter-City Director John Prideaux "gets with it" to the music of Gerry Marsden backed by the Searchers at Lime Street Station. *Peter Fox*

▶Radio 1's 'Gary Davis Show' was broadcast from the mv 'IRIS'. The DJ is seen here in hippy guise. *Peter Fox*

◀"Instant" Cyril Bleasdale, the L.M. Region General Manager enjoys himself with five specially-chartered mini-skirted models! *Peter Fox*

►The updated image of InterCity – HST power car 43072 sports the revised livery with the yellow cut back to small areas of the front end and cab roof only. The new-style bodyside logo, whilst stylish, also curiously removed one of the best-known cliches 'InterCity 125'.

Peter Fox

◄"See a friend this weekend" proclaimed the '60s ad. Model "Monica" now living in Switzerland returned to England at BR's request for the InterCity 21 celebrations and is seen here posing in front of her famous poster. *Peter Fox*

▼The ten surviving 1966 West Coast Main Line Pullman cars have undergone a £50,000 refit to become part of the InterCity charter fleet. An important change is the fitting of air brakes, but they can still only be hauled by a.c. electric locos. Renamed *Crummock Water* after a Lakeland beauty spot, parlour first 553 is seen at Carlisle station on 20th May. *John Augustson*

▲The full fleet of 85 Class 150/2 Sprinter DMUs with front-end corridor connections became operational during 1988, mainly on Trans-Pennine workings, but also in South Wales and southern Scotland. The attempt to completely dispense with the yellow painted end, shown in this view of No. 150 239 at Helsby on 23rd April, was quickly abandoned in favour of the normal blanket coating of yellow warning paint.   *Duncan Street.*

▼The Skippers that became slippers..... The chocolate and cream Class 142 railbuses were as much a disaster in the West Country as their Provincial sisters based in the North West and Tyneside. A succession of failures of the Self Changing Gears transmissions, wheel defects and tyre wear on tight curves were a nightmare. Many units were stored pending repair, and old units kept in service beyond their expected lives. Cornish sets Nos. 142 016 and 142 027, seen leaving Barnstaple Junction for Exeter on 3rd August, are now at Neville Hill and Newton Heath respectively.   *Les Nixon.*

PROVINCIAL

The terms Provincial Services and Sprinter Revolution were inextricably linked during 1987, because what should have been a year of prosperity between the new partnership was another rather damp squib based on trying to do too much too soon.

The shop window was the much-neglected Trans-Pennine route between Scarborough and Holyhead (235 miles), which from May was handed over to £10 million worth of Class 150/2 Sprinter DMUs with outstanding mechanical success, but less favourable public reaction because of acute overcrowding on many services, and the unsuitability of the seating layout for such long-distance services. Loco-hauled services over the 179 miles from Newcastle to Liverpool were increased to a two hourly frequency.

Elsewhere, many of the plans went awry because of late deliveries of rolling stock, and defects with that already available.

The Cardiff area of South Wales also joined the Sprinter revolution from the 5th October timetable revisions to reflect a 50 per cent increase in passenger traffic in just four years. However, teething troubles with stock and timings took the shine off the massive investment authorised for the area.

▲This certainly wasn't in Provincial's plans, but the desperation caused by the halting of much of the Class 142/143 Pacer DMU fleet with transmission and wheel faults forced the return of loco-hauled services in the North East. One such working, the 1718 Newcastle–Berwick, is easy work for Class 47/4 No. 47422 at Alnmouth on 4th September.

Stephen Miller

▼The 30-year-old Metro-Cammell units like the one in the foreground embarrassingly proved more reliable than their new-tech replacements sharing the same platform at Skipton on 7th February. Couple that to complaints about severe overcrowding on the modern types, and you can understand why Provincial Services will not look back on 1987 with affection.

Les Nixon

In the South West, the short reign of the attractive brown and cream Class 142 Pacer DMUs had to be curtailed because of severe tyre wear as they squealed around the tight curves. Back came stock that had started life in the same location 30 years before.

Critical shortages of new stock in the Manchester and Newcastle areas, also the fault of gearbox and wheel faults with Class 142s and 143s, also meant another cobbling together of fit-for-scrap units which brought threats of legal action and withdrawal of subsidies by metropolitan authorities already digging deep into their pockets with subsidies.

The 10-mile Coventry–Nuneaton route were reopened on 11th May, with the target of setting up a new through Coventry–Nottingham service.

And what of the Settle and Carlisle? Well, very little really, except admissions during October that the route was one of the best financial performers in Provincial Services. The expected decision on its future didn't materialise, although resistance did strengthen, and BR joined local authorities in a highly successful promotion campaign.

▲Operating costs on Trans-Pennine routes were slashed with the introduction of Class 150/2 Sprinter DMUs. No. 150 238 leads the 09.53 Scarborough–Liverpool/Holyhead through Diggle on 10th April three weeks before the type's squadron introduction with the May timetable. *Rodney Lissenden.*

►A distinct feeling of deja-vu at Dawlish on 4th October. The varied body profiles of Class 142 replacement stock in transit from the West Midlands to Plymouth makes it look distinctly second-hand. *Colin Marsden*

◄Leyland's 155 Super Sprinters was another story of delays. Deliveries fell well behind schedule, and barely a dozen of the 35 two-car units were in use by the year end. West Yorkshire PTE took the rare step of ordering seven extra units without going through BR's conventional tendering procedure. Unit No. 155 303, allocated to Cardiff, is seen at Droitwich Spa on a Worcester Shrub Hill–Birmingham New Street working on 10th October. *Les Nixon*

▲A last look at a Class 142 Skipper unit in Cornwall, as unit No. 142 027 stands at Coombe Junction on the scenic Liskeard–Looe branch on 22nd April. Its chocolate and cream livery is now somewhat out of place on Manchester suburban duties!   *Les Nixon.*

►Passengers in North Wales were far from happy. First, squealing flanges on the tight curves of the Conwy Valley branch to Blaenau Ffestiniog forced the removal of Class 142 and 150 DMUs from 29th June. Second, the ex-Tyseley Class 116 units drafted in as replacements were slammed for their filthy condition. DMS 53123 leads the formation of the 16.10 ex-Llandudno into Betws-y-Coed on 2nd July.   *Larry Goddard.*

◀Conwy station (closed 14th February 1966) was put back on the map on 27th June when a completely new station was reopened with the backing of Gwynedd County Council. Sprinter No. 150 251 is pictured taking VIPs back to Bangor after the opening ceremony.

Larry Goddard.

◀Although increasingly used for passenger diversions and special traffic, the Nuneaton–Coventry freight route was officially upgraded in May, although without intermediate stations for the time being. On 25th May, Class 116 DMU formed 53075+53835 pass Three Spires Junction with the 14.56 Stafford–Coventry. The unit was withdrawn before the year end.

Paul Shannon.

▼Rotherham started the year with one station, and finished up with two. Completion of the Holmes Chord linking the former Midland main line with the parallel Great Central route enabled the opening of the new Central station for the start of the May timetable, although nearby Masborough on the main line remained in use while a public inquiry considered objections. A Class 101 unit is seen entering Central on 12th May.

Les Nixon.

►The design is hardly a stunning award winner, but the rebirth of Birmingham Snow Hill station is an important feature of the current West Midlands PTA passenger strategy, which includes a restored tunnel and cross-city link to Smethwick. The old structure, closed on 4th March 1972, became labelled the world's largest unstaffed halt. The new one, costing £7.4 million, may eventually go over to LRT operation. The picture is dated 12th March.

Steven Knight.

►The outdated, cramped, and awkwardly-sited Birmingham Moor Street was a victim of the Snow Hill project, replaced by a new halt alongside the old Great Western structure. There is a distinct period flavour of this 31st January view of stock on services to Leamington Spa and Stratford-on-Avon, and the structure may survive as a museum.

Les Nixon.

▼West Midlands PTA chairman Peter Lister used 2nd October's opening ceremony to publicly tell BR chairman Sir Robert Reid he was stock. Otherwise, the event heralded a massive success for the new rail link. On 5th October, the first day of regular services, Class 116 unit Nos. 53826+59329+53905 enters Show Hill tunnel with the 13.52 service to Leamington Spa.

Stephen Widdowson.

NETWORK SOUTH-EAST

Network SouthEast had every reason to celebrate its first full year. A massive upturn in business, new electric lines, stations rebuilt and modernised, and above all, a new public image.

The jewels in the crown were undoubtedly the full inauguration in May of the Hitchin–Peterborough and Bishops Stortford–Cambridge electric extensions, followed by Sanderstead–East Grinstead during October.

The GN electric extension is seen as one of NSE's greatest passenger growth areas, boosted by massive population increases en-route. The same applies at Cambridge, where permission was also given during 1987 to electrify the, "missing link" loop north of Royston.

On the Southern, the Sanderstead–East Grinstead electric services were inaugurated during October, resulting in better stock utilisation, and another upturn in passenger traffic. Attention is now being turned into modernising the nearby Uckfield branch, although not with the addition of a third rail.

More rurally, Corby rejoined the rail map. Construction of a new halt to serve a shuttle paytrain service to Kettering was so successful in its early days that guards were unable to collect all the fares in the short journey time. Electrification largely rests on the creation of the proposed Wonderworld leisure complex at Corby in the early 1990s.

Of the many freight lines in the Home Counties currently under study for passenger re-openings, the Oxford–Bicester line was reborn amid much razzmatazz on 9th May, and the hope is that the full route to Bletchley and Milton Keynes will follow before long.

►The service may be modest, but patronage of the Kettering–Corby shuttle service was so heavy that guards could not collect the fares in the short time journey time. Electrification of this service may follow if the proposed Wonderworld leisure park gets off the ground. On 21st July, unit No. 51572 + 59163 + 51912 arrives at Corby with the 10.26 ex-Kettering service.

Paul Shannon.

◄And where are the Class 310s going? To the Great Eastern and LTS where 1958-design Class 302 stock will fall out of the bottom. It was careful planning that meant only NSE-liveried stock was sent across in the opening months. Unit No. 310 084 stands at Liverpool Street on 22nd September.

Iain C. Scotchman.

►The shift-round of NSE stock started to bring benefits to the Euston–Birmingham line when 1981-build Class 317 units displaced from the Bedford line started to replace Class 310s which have been in charge for more than two decades. Unit No. 317 323, in NSE livery, was at Birmingham International on 30th December. *Steven Knight*

◄Electric services from Bishops Stortford north to Cambridge started without ceremony on 19th January and the new May timetable promised 2000 extra seats per day to London. The glamourous side of the new service was Class 86 haulage. The VIP run was postponed three months because of bad weather. Loco No. 86401, specially repainted in NSE livery, stands at Cambridge on 23rd March, having made a 47 min record run from Liverpool Street. *Brian Morrison*

◄The less glamorous side of the Cambridge electrification scheme – the Class 305 and 308 units drafted in were considerably older than the hauled stock they replaced. And the trouble was, the passengers rumbled it. As the year progressed, NSE announced plans to build 30 Class 321 sets for Great Eastern Lines at a cost of £39 million. Unit No. 305 503 leaves Broxbourne with the 10.25 Cambridge–London on 15th August. *Alex Dasi-Sutton.*

▼The three-year renovation of London's Fenchurch Street terminus, used by 65 000 Southend line commuters each weekday, was completed on September 22, but behind the £3 million refurbished 1854 frontage and platforms is a much grander £28.5 million office and shops development. This view is dated 22nd November. *Rodney Lissenden.*

The six miles from Watford Junction to St Albans Abbey, one of the last leafy branch lines north of London, was approved on July 16 for a £675,000 electric facelift.

Its future secured, work started on facelifting the somewhat shabby Chiltern Line, which were incidentally handed over the Western Region from 4th October. It has started with a clean-up at Marylebone, while down the line there will be track replacement, new signalling and station modernisation. A new station was created at Haddenham and Thame Parkway.

The Isle of Wight, long the Cinderella of the Southern Region, gained a new £80,000 station at Lake, plus a hint that its pre-war rolling stock might soon be replaced by "new" ex-LT Central Line 1962 stock. There is also talk of BR helping with the £500,000 of re-establishing the Wootton–Smallbrook route to connect the tourist line at Smallbrook Junction.

London's 1854 Fenchurch Street station was reopened on 22nd September after its £3 million facelift. The Grade 1 listed frontage has been incorporated into a completely redesigned structure that now is now just a small part of a £28.5 million office and shops complex.

Behind the scenes, the first trains were run through the Snow Hill tunnel which will allow Bedford–Brighton through services from May 1988. Further afield, Weymouth's 20-year isolation from the Bournemouth electric link was closer to ending with the arrival of the first luxury Class 442 rolling stock from BREL Derby.

Sector Director Chris Green was congratulated on the success of his clean-up campaign. Smarter stations, stock cleaner inside and out, greater punctuality and better staff service have reached the heart of most commuters.

The statistics of NSE operation continue to be staggering – 2,500 route miles (75% of them electrified), and 935 stations.

NSE has 1.4 million passenger journeys each weekday, 420,000 of them in the peak periods alone. The rolling stock total is 6760 vehicles, 5960 of them EMUs, 386 DMUs, 60 locomotives, and 354 hauled coaches.

Income for 1987–88 rose to £710 million, a nine per cent increase on 1986/87. At the same time, Government support dropped by £51 million to £196 million. Investment planned for the next five years is £952 million. Rolling stock will cost £383 million, stations £172 million, signalling

▲Mass repainting of rolling stock left the multi-coloured NSE trademark everywhere during 1987, even down to the humblest single car DMU. This picture of two ex-works Class 121s at Doncaster on 3rd October shows the contrast. On the right, a light overhaul on No. 55028 leaves it in blue and grey. On the left, full NSE garb has been applied to No. 55020, which incidentally was in GWR chocolate and cream for the 1985 anniversary celebrations.

Les Nixon.

▼Locomotives and complete rakes of rolling stock entered into the NSE spirit – well, almost. A single blue and grey Mark 2 coach next to Class 50 No. 50005 *Collingwood* spoils the consistency of the 11.10 Waterloo–Exeter at Wimbledon on 23rd October. The loco's livery has been revised from the original NSE paint style.

Colin Marsden.

£122 million, electrification £39 million, and other items £196 million.

If much of the red, white and blue rolling stock was still mutton dressed as lamb, the arrival of the first Class 319 'Thameslink' stock on the Bedford–St Pancras line allowed other 25 kV routes to benefit from spare stock. Thus it was that 317s were cascaded to the Euston–Northampton line, 310s to the Great Eastern. NSE promised better to come by ordering 46 replacement Class 321 EMUs for the Cambridge line, and 14 further Thameslink units to cope with expected demand. The new North Kent and South Essex 'Networker' design even reached the formal design stage, although not expected to replace life-expired Class 415 4 EPB and Class 302s until at least 1992.

▲BR's oldest active coaching stock is also getting the NSE touch. On the Isle of Wight, some of the ex-London Transport coaches are 65 years old, but far from pensioned off. Ex-works at Ryde St Johns on 25th February were two coaches of set No. 485 045.   *Hugh Ballantyne.*

▼The new image multiple unit that never really made it. Paxman-engined DEMU No. 210 002 ran its final days out of Reading depot in 1987 before joining its sister unit No. 210 001 at Derby Technical Centre. The design, with engine above the frames, was soon considered too lavish for non InterCity services and subsequent designs reverted to underfloor power units. The body fo/ed the basis of the class 317 EMUs. On 21st August No. 210 002 forms the 18.01 Bedwyn–Reading service at Colthrop.   *Paul Shannon.*

PARCELS

▲The Parcels Sector was more stable after several years of contraction, although loco-hauled services continued to give way to reconditioned former passenger DMUs. An example of this change was the final run of a TPO through Worcester Shrub Hill on 16th January when Class 45/1 No. 45149 carried a special headboard. The local mail is now sent on a local DMU from Cheltenham.   *Stephen Widdowson.*

▼A new parcels service introduced during 1987 was the 1M85 1238 Gillingham–Preston, seen here at New Hythe behind Class 33 No. 33028 on 6th July.   *Paul Shannon.*

BR's Parcels Sector worked hard to shake off its poor-relation image during 1987, a reputation gained after several years of severe recession from loss of traffic and heavy operating deficits.

Spare siding space littered with redundant parcels vans was happily not repeated as Parcels got to grips with its business by increasing utilisation and cutting costs.

Newspaper distribution was effectively halved when BR admitted defeat in its fight to retain Mirror Group business. The offer of collecting papers from print works was outlawed because BR is not allowed to run road vehicles and employ drivers. This was the second major blow to the system, News International having gone over to road in 1985.

Red Star went International, with an offer of collection from the sender and delivery to customers in the United States, often the same day. The plan is to extend the service to the whole of Europe.

On 3rd September, Northern Ireland Railways were completely integrated into the Red Star service by means of a new computerised system which also enables monitoring of the package during its entire journey.

Traction wise, Parcels chose two depots to maintain its fleet of 90 locomotives, Class 47/4s at Bristol Bath Road, and Class 31/4s at Crewe. Under the wires, Parcels chose the option of financing five of the new Class 90 electric locos, while hiring others for overnight work.

Conversion of DMUs for specialist parcels traffic continued, albeit very slowly. The concept is still to replace small loco-hauled trains with two-car diesel units, in multiple if necessary.

Depots at Cambridge, Cardiff Canton, Longsight and Tyseley were being prepared to maintain the sector's DMU (or DPU) fleet, with Ilford providing back up for the handful of electric-powered vehicles.

With the cost of new Sprinter-type units ruled out on cost grounds, attention has been centred on redundant ex-Lincoln "Derby Heavyweight" Class 114 units, which need roller-shutter doors. One has been experimentally equipped with 205 hp Leyland TL11 engines as fitted to new railbuses.

Former Bedford–St Pancras Class 127 units, also rescued from the

▲The Parcels Sector made some medium-term investment in purpose-rebuilt Class 114 two-car parcels units, with renovated interiors and fitting of roller shutter doors. The work being undertaken at Ilford depot. 53040 receives the treatment on 23rd October 1987. *Brian Morrison.*

▼At the other end of the spectrum, cast-offs were still employed. At Kings Cross on 24th April, work-weary Class 120 car No. 53739 (withdrawn in August) partners Class 105 No. 53365 with an overnight parcels working to Cambridge. Only two Class 120 parcels units remained in traffic at the end of the year, working from Chester. *Iain Scotchman.*

scrapheap, were also being considered for a complete engine and transmission transplant. Class 128 single car survivors were authorised for asbestos removal.

While all this planning was going on, Parcels continued to operate with increasingly decrepit cast-offs that included asbestos-contaminated Cravens Class 105 units that with one exception (non-asbestos) were completely taken off passenger duties in May.

Hauled stock is maintained at a variety of locations, and like the rest of the sector's fleet is now conspicuous by its lack of corporate identity, bar the occasional red stripe across the solid blue. One exception, however was Parcels sector allocated Class 47 loco 47522 painted in LNER Apple Green with parcels logo to give the Doncaster BRML open day some extra sparkle.

Parcels had yet to show its true colours.

RAILFREIGHT

Why should freight trains be dirty? Smart, colourful and above all clean locomotives and stock were seen as an important feature of Railfreight's aggressive marketing campaign.

Railfreight's determination to gain prosperity was marked by an October exhibition which showed how this slimmed-down sector is ready to take on all-comers.

Where it really mattered, Railfreight made some remarkable strides in its continued recovery from the effects of the disastrous coal strike two years previously. Profit for 1986–87 was £24.7 million surplus before repayment of interest, well on the way to achieving its stipulated 5% return on assets by 1988/89.

The success has come by way of cutting costs, better stock utilisation and big savings in manpower by means of one-man operation.

Although still in its relatively early stages, dedication of locomotives and rolling stock to specific sub-sectors paid great dividends both in reliability and customer confidence. Metals and Automotive, Speedlink, Coal, Petroleum and Construction traffic patterns were clearly identified for the first time.

Domestic coal traffic was recognised as an almost totally separate business from July with the completion of a new sub-sector virtually divorced from the rest of the Speedlink system. Principal yards are at Millerhill (Edinburgh), Healey Mills (Wakefield), Toton (Nottingham), Washwood Heath (Birmingham), Didcot, Radyr (Cardiff), and Pantyfynnon, with radiating services as appropriate.

On a smaller scale, there were many successes in both securing and generating new freight business; alumina from Blyth to Fort William; fish from Mallaig to Grimsby; timber from Kyle of Lochalsh; grain from East Anglia; oil from Thame and Cleveland; and cider from Hereford.

Private interest was shown in creating a new north–south freight route without resort to public money, and without the additional height-restriction of 25 kV overhead electric wires. The GW route to Birmingham, Settle and Carlisle, and GSW Carlisle–Glasgow lines would then assume a key new role.

BR ignored its hitherto hard and fast policy of encouraging private-owner wagons by ordering for itself from BREL Doncaster 124 high-capacity 46-tonne china clay wagons for the prospering Cornwall china clay traffic.

Freightliners faced up to reality and closed eight of its depots, but stressed its increasing role in the Continental container business at Felixstowe and other ports.

A sizeable victim of progress into fixed train formations was Severn Tunnel Junction yard, which was axed completely in favour of smaller siding space at East Usk (Newport) and Gloucester. A small number of freight branches also fell by the wayside.

Congestion at Felixstowe's container port was eased from February with the opening of a new £2 million spur from the mainline which enabled trains to complete a circuit instead or reversing through the congested docks area.

The Trailer Train, Maxilink and Minilink rail/road systems were unveiled, following, again, the broad principle that customers want one invoice for delivery of Speedlink goods from the maunfacturer to the doorstep.

Minilink and Maxilink were two sizes of demountable bogies which employed a four-wheel road chassis to switch containers for road to rail in a few seconds. The Trailer train places an articulated road trailer onto a set of rail wheels.

Dark clouds on the horizon however were the effects of privatisation – would a privatised electricity industry reorganise its coal purchases without rail? Apart from some localised successes, bulk commodity rail traffic also showed little prospect of major growth.

Locomotives in particular began to adopt a whole new look with a livery of grey and yellow that was personalised with colourful sub-sector symbols, plus cast plaques to indicate depot ownership.

On its cleaner image, Railfreight has even written to customers asking them to clean up their private-owner wagons.

Finally, there was still place for nostalgia. September saw Railfreight chiefs musing over a 1950s style vintage freight train of renovated vacuum-braked vehicles to demonstrate the enormous developments that have taken place in the last three decades.

◄ Felixstowe's Northern Freightliner Terminal was given a more direct link with the main line from 16th February with the opening of the mile-long spur from Trimley, using the old crossing loop for access to BR property. The more circuitous route crossing a main road and dock lanes is now less used. The picture shows Class 47 No. 47346 at the terminal on 21st November, having run round its overnight service from Coatbridge. It will now draw forward to reverse and gain access to the terminal.   *Michael Collins.*

▲Eight major Freightliner depots were slated for closure in a January 9 report designed to re-shape the company into two sections, one for haulage of deep sea containers from the ports to inland terminals, and the other for European markets and UK long-haul domestic traffic. A poorly-loaded 4V73 Cardiff-bound liner train leaves Follingsby (Newcastle) on 19th January. This terminal closed in April – others axed were Aberdeen, Dundee, Edinburgh, Hull, Manchester Longsight, Nottingham and Swansea. *Michael Rhodes.*

▼One yard with a buoyant business base is Ripple Lane on London's east side, and BR has invested heavily in a fleet of modernised locos to handle the heavy fuel traffic.Class 37 No. 37889 demonstrates its correct sector ownership as it leaves with the 6V52 1445 Langley tanks on 22nd December. Next to it is No. 37893 on the following 6M32 1501 Ripple Lane–Thame tanks. *Paul Shannon.*

A familiar view, but now no more. The last rites of Severn Tunnel Junction freight yard were performed on 10th October after 151 years. A victim of freight cutbacks and containerisation, its remaining traffic is now handled by other local yards including East Usk (Newport) and Gloucester. It seemed to be business as usual however on 9th July, with loco Nos. 56050, 47377 and 47308 all ready to depart.
Michael Rhodes.

◀Further west, Margam hump yard also closed in October. Covering 120 acres, it was only 25 years old and the last to be built under the 1955 freight plan. The picture shows Class 37 No. 37285 leaving on the 6C60 Margam–Llynfi Junction/Cardiff Tidal Sidings empties on 31st March. There is however some brighter news for the area – see picture below.
Michael Rhodes.

▼From May engineers removed four miles of track and numerous turnouts from the old Margam yard for installation at a more suitable site nearby. Eleven of the 18 roads at Knuckle Yard will link directly with the BSC Port Talbot plant, which with a million tonnes of steel a year and inward traffic of lime and coal will form the lion's share of the yard's 85 trains a week. This was construction work on 10th August.
Brian Morrison.

A new container terminal at Ellesmere Port was opened in February as Northern Ireland-based coal exporters Cawoods decided to modernise, and withdraw from Swansea Docks where coal hoists and vacuum-braked wagons were life-expired. Rail traffic now operates direct to Briton Ferry, and Class 37 No. 37897 has charge of one such train on 17th February.
David Rapson.

►Regular use of Class 58s on the 10.20 Didcot–Chessington coal trains was like using a sledgehammer to crack a nut, but a popular enthusiast spectator event. No. 58022 arrives at Chessington South coal terminal with 12 hoppers on 23rd October – but how many are loaded?
Colin Marsden.

►Freight traffic is rare at the southern end of the East Coast Main Line, so a short-term contract to convey pipes from Leith was most welcome. The tiny yard at St Neots was used for offloading. The train is seen at Tyne Yard in the charge of Class 47/0 No. 47006 on 30th June.
Michael Rhodes.

▲One of the final vacuum-braked revenue earning freights, the daily Marks Tey–Mile End Tarmac sand train, saw the year out before modernisation with new vehicles. Normally a duty for two Class 31/1s, it was entrusted to Class 47/0 No. 47014 on 11th August, seen at Marks Tey. *Michael Collins.*

▼Freight returned the Copy Pit route on 7th July after a gap of several years, but only just! Class 37/0 No. 37057 crosses the viaduct at Cornholme on 6th August with the 6M76 08.11 Healey Mills–Preston Deepdale Speedlink. *Paul Shannon.*

▲Into the 1990s with Railfreight. A radical new livery also features a large bodyside emblem to indicate its sub-sector allocation. This is Petroleum managed 37892 prior to its naming *Ripple Lane* at the London depot on 19th October. *Steven Knight.*

►A new road-rail initiative launched by Railfreight includes specially equipped lorries which can visit a container depot and load themselves without the need for a crane. Two of the four prototypes were on show at Ripple Lane on 19th October, and operate between Willesden and Deanside Transit at Hillingdon, Glasgow. *Steven Knight.*

►Large numbers of locomotives were still out-shopped in the old Railfreight livery, but the somewhat drab all-over grey was considerably brightened up by the addition of broad red stripe around the lower bodysides and across the bufferbeam. This was Class 47/3 No. 47301, ex-works at Doncaster on 3rd October. *David Masterman.*

▲Class 86/4 No. 86401 was uniquely painted in Network South-East livery to launch the Bishops Stortford–Cambridge electrification extension on 19th January, but was like a fish out of water when bad weather cancelled the event. The loco spent the year on its time-honoured West Coast duties, looking somewhat out of place at Glasgow Central! It was even more out of place, but nevertheless a welcome exhibit at the Basingstoke open day on 27th September. Behind it is another electric loco., former Manchester–Sheffield and Nederlandse Spoorwegen Class EM2 No. 1502 (27000) *ELECTRA*   *Howard Johnston*

▼New Railfreight sector livery was applied to Class 50 No. 50149 *Defiance* during fitting of overhauled bogies and modified traction motors at Laira during the autumn. After trials it was moved to St. Blazey for china clay work and is pictured there.   *Brian Denton*

LOCOMOTIVES

▶What started off 1987 as a Class 87/2 ended the year as a Class 90 when BR considered there would be more prestige attached to its expensive new a.c. electric if they were not associated with the 14-year-old design they were evolved from. The loco was not ready in time for its expected naming by The Queen during her visit to BREL Crewe Works as this 4th July open day view of No 87201 shows.

John Gosling

▼The same loco, now redesignated 90001, was outshopped from BREL Crewe on 31st October. It ran commissioning trials to Winsford, and by 14th December, the date of this photo, was undergoing tests at Derby Technical Centre. Note the different buffers, and InterCity livery with "anti-enthusiast" small numbers on the lower bodysides.

Colin Marsden

Although no formal contract was signed for the proposed fleet of 100 Class 60 diesel freight locomotives, most of BR's 1987 traction plan was based around them.

But there were some other important developments during the year, including the full implementation of sector ownership, a completely revised maintenance policy, rundown of many older types in anticipation of squadron introduction of Sprinter DMUs and electrification, and two new electric designs themselves.

As the year progressed, the entire fleet was split between the five BR business sectors, or to departmental use. It was a simple financial exercise to define costs, and every effort was made to allocate specific locos to particular traffic, hence the simultaneous emergence of the sub-sector.

In October, yet another livery scheme was introduced, whereby Railfreight engines would be immediately identifiable by a new three-tone grey colour scheme with badges to indicate home base, and whether dedicated to general work, coal, petroleum, distribution, construction, or metals traffic.

InterCity took over some Class 47/4s, 73s, 81s, 82s, 83s, 85s, 86s, 87s and an 89, and maintained them at Crewe Diesel, Eastfield, Old Oak Common, Bristol Bath Road, Stewarts Lane, Shields Road, Crewe Electric, and Willesden.

Provincial handled 31/4s, 33/0s, 37/4s, 47/4s, 47/7s and 50s at Bescot, Crewe Diesel, Stratford, Eastfield, Inverness, Cardiff, Gateshead, Bristol Bath Road, and Laira.

Network SouthEast looked after a handful of 33/1s, 47/4s, 50s, 73s, 85s and 86/4s at Eastleigh, Stratford, Old Oak Common, Laira, Stewarts Lane, Willesden and Crewe Electric.

Railfreight, the biggest user, maintained 20s, 26s, 31s, 33s, 37s, 45s, 47s, 50s, 56s, 58s, 73s, 85s, 86s, and 87s at Toton, Immingham, Thornaby, Haymarket, Tinsley, Stratford, Eastleigh, Stewarts Lane, Eastfield, Motherwell, Inverness, Cardiff, Crewe Diesel, Laira, Crewe Electric and Willesden.

Parcels had but a few 31/4s, 33s, 45/1s, 47/4s, 50s, 73s, 81s, 85s, 86s, and 87s allocated to Old Oak Common, Bristol Bath Road, March, Immingham, Eastleigh, Stewarts Lane, Tinsley, Gateshead, Crewe Diesel, Stratford, Laira, Shields Road, Crewe Electric and Willesden.

Maintenance is explained in detail earlier in this book.

Three time-honoured loco classes went completely to the wall during 1987. March saw the demise of the last of the 1250 hp Sulzer-engined BR-design Class 25 Bo–Bos, which once numbered 327 examples and were a common sight from Inverness to Penzance. Overhauls ceased six years before, and Crewe became their last home. Only four months later, Scotland rid itself of its similar Birmingham RC&W Class 27 design, a somewhat curious decision as many had only been completely rebuilt at Glasgow Works two years previously. As the year drew to a close, there was also a quiet exit for 82008, the last Beyer Peacock built loco in capital stock, which had outlived the rest of the class for some time on Euston ECS duty.

Major inroads were also made into other classes. The BR design Class 45 "Peaks" were little short of decimated, while severe cash limits on maintenance and accident repairs saw many hitherto "safe" Class 20s, 31s, 33s and 47s consigned to the scrapheap. The first Class 50 locomotive to be withdrawn was 50011 *Centurion* at the beginning of the year to become a test bed

for overhauled power units at Crewe Works. Indeed, there might have been far more withdrawals but for the problems encountered with Sprinter and Pacer DMUs. Class 47/4s became a common sight on three Mark 1 coaches in the North East, while on the Western Region first generation DMUs were frequently towed out of trouble by Class 31s, 33s and 37s.

The success story was the dedicated Class 37 fleet whose availability for traffic hit new heights. Even so, Railfreight's cash flow saw the number to be refurbished slashed in favour of lower-cost intermediate overhauls with just refurbished CP7 bogies. The humble Class 26s, many of which celebrated their 30th birthdays, were rewarded with visits to works for further life extension for the 1990s.

It was too early to form opinions of the new Brush Class 89 Co–Co electric, which appeared just before the end of 1986, although it did undergo extensive trials on the West Coast Main Line. Class 90, the new name for the re-worked Class 87, emerged from Crewe Works during December, but 'Electra' 91001 was still in undercoat alongside.

One of the big disappointments of 1987 was the lack of success of Railfreight's experimental Class 50. After months of expectation, 50149 *Defiance* was fitted with replacement bogies and regeared traction motors, but failed to impress WR officials hoping for a high-adhesion alternative to the Class 56 in the West Country. No more will be converted.

Doncaster's very last diesel loco 58050 was fitted with separately excited traction motors, and spent most of the year either in store, on test from Toton, or parked at Stratford undergoing repaint into new sector livery.

Foster Yeoman's General Motors Class 59s continued to give good and reliable service, a few wheel defects apart, and consideration was given to ordering a fifth example. Surprisingly, no other similar firms took the plunge and ordered their own locomotive fleets.

Plans for the new class 60 freight locomotive were unveiled during the year with tenders being issued for the supply of 100 locomotives over a four year period. A mock-up of the cab was produced and was exhibited at the Ripple Lane Railfreight exhibition.

The shunter fleet saw little change because of the concentration of resources on the main line fleet. Even so, the increasing availability of spare dual and air-braked 350 hp Class 08s allowed the elimination of the smaller 204 hp Class 03s from Colchester, Norwich and Gateshead, leaving just three to work at Birkenhead. Class 09 also suffered its first withdrawal when 09017 was commandeered for the Severn Tunnel emergency train.

And what of nostalgia? This was reserved mainly for pioneer Class 40 D 200, which hauled specials to all parts of the country during the warm months, but lack of suitable steam-heat coaching stock saw it relegated to mundane freight and departmental activity for the rest of the time. At the end of the year, transfer to Crewe with the rundown of Carlisle Kingmoor saw it allocated to wholly new, but still obscure duties.

Sister D 335 became a star itself. First withdrawn in January 1985 and only hours from the torch at Doncaster, it was rescued for departmental traffic, and in January 1987 consigned to Swindon, again for scrap. It only reached Gloucester yard, and after retrieval was lovingly restored by Tyseley depot and exhibited around the country. It was also put back into running order, and with similarly reprieved Class 27 loco 27059 was even used on passenger duties at the autumn Severn

▶The very last locomotive to be built at BREL Doncaster Works before its transformation into a BR Level Five maintenance depot and central spares centre was Class 58 No. 58050 during March, also the only machine from The Plant to carry a 1987 worksplate. It was fitted with separately excited ("Sepex") traction motors for better adhesion, and thus spent most of the year on trial. 9th May saw it named *Toton Traction Depot* at the Nottingham coal loco centre's open day. It was then used as a testbed for the new Railfreight coal livery, and spent several weeks out of traffic before being unveiled to the unsuspecting freight customer at an exhibition at Ripple Lane depot. Note the cast bodyside depot symbol, coal markings, and nameplate moved higher up the cabside. Photo date: 15th October.

Steven Knight

Valley Railway diesel event.

Another pioneer to escape the scrapman for the second time was Class 14 diesel-hydraulic D 9500, which along with the rest of the working survivors at the British Coal plant at Ashington, Northumberland were snapped up by preservationists to take the total to a staggering 19 – not bad for a build of only 56 that was considered one of BR's greatest white elephants with only three years work after completion at Swindon Works in 1965.

Undoubtedly the saddest and perhaps best recorded sight came as a result of the rapid sale of withdrawn Class 25s and 27s to Vic Berry's scrapyard at Leicester for breaking up. They arrived in such numbers from BREL Swindon, and Crewe Gresty Lane that they outstripped Berry's demolition capacity, and over 30 bodies were stacked three high to the delight of media and enthusiast photographers alike. The sight may well be repeated during 1988 with so many redundant assets heading in the same direction.

◀ The Brush-designed electric Co–Co prototype Class 89 No. 89001 made its first tentative trips under its own power from Crewe to Hartford on 20th February, having been subjected to tests at both Loughborough and Derby. Test running proper began in mid-April between Crewe, Willesden, Carlisle and Speke, mostly with the BREL International train, and a production batch has still not been ruled out as a fall-back option if the Class 91 is unsuccessful, as well as for the Channel Tunnel. The loco is seen at Speke Junction on 28th April.

David Rapson

▼Despite a good deal of debate, the decision on who is going to build BR's new-generation Class 60 freight locos was not actually taken during 1987. A closing date of 6th November was set for receipt of tenders from six invited consortia, with the first 2900–3250 h.p., 95% availability, 35% adhesion, loco delivered by March 1989, and the entire fleet of 100 over a period of four years. Two wooden mock-ups of front end design were made, and this one was chosen as the best. It was displayed at Ripple Lane on 17th October.

Michael Collins

◄Sectorisation of the Class 37 fleet really took a hold during 1987 as refurbishment and other overhauls was followed by despatch for specific duties. There was no mistaking No. 37501 *Teesside Steelmaster* from February when it was painted in British Steel house colours of light blue. It is pictured partnering No. 37502 *British Steel Teesside* past Westhouses on the Erewash Valley line on 23rd April in charge of a special Lackenby–Corby coil steel train.

John Tuffs

◄*Thornaby Demon* plates were unofficially attached to Class 37/5 No. 37512 to reflect its special characteristics. As a "demonstrator" loco, it spent most of the summer at Derby Technical Centre, and was photographed at Gloucester depot on 25th September.

Norman Preedy

▼Class 37/5 and 37/7 overhauls continued at Crewe as finance allowed, while the last of the trio with Ruston RK270T power units No. 37906 ran on test along the North Wales line on 16th March. The scene is Llandudno Junction, where it was derailed on another run-out on 3rd April after rectification.

Larry Goddard

►BR's 20-year aim to fit air brakes to its entire mainline locomotive fleet was finally achieved with entry into Doncaster Works on 8th January of Class 31/1 No. 31271, the only machine not fitted with air brakes. It emerged in the modified Railfreight livery that was to typify all Class 31s outshopped during the year – grey bodysides, but wide red band around the entire lower bodysides. By then transferred from Kingmoor depot to Bescot, 31271 leaves the exchange sidings at Wednesbury on 22nd May with three departmental wagons carrying test weights from the steel terminal.
Paul Shannon

►The loss of locomotive No. 31436 in the 1986 Chinley accident prompted BREL Doncaster to bring the Class 31/4 fleet total back up to quota with the ETH equipment transferred to the next refurbishment loco off the production line. Thus, 31277 became 31469 at the end of the number series, and emerged in the second week of January in blue livery instead of Railfreight grey. (It was out of traffic again within days with minor collision damage).
Les Nixon

▼The Class 31/4 sub-class was ironically and sadly depleted again on 20th February when No. 31440 was written off in yet another collision at Chinley when the 16.22 Sheffield–Liverpool struck an overloaded limestone train from Peak Forest which overran catch points. This was the scene of the accident with Class 47 loco No. 47089 and its mangled freight wagons in the foreground. This time, there was no 31470.
Peter Fox

◄The Class 25 locomotive fleet had shrunk so small by early March to allow complete eradication and replacement by other types. Most were in poor condition because they had lasted six or seven years without works overhaul, but were involved on trip workings in the North West and southern Scotland even beyond the withdrawal deadline of Sunday 15th March. Looking work-stained but still capable of a good day's work, No. 25323 has only a few weeks work left in it as it arrives at Crewe on 29th January with a trip working from Radway Green to Basford Hall. It was one of the many examples quickly sold to Vic Berry of Leicester, and was scrapped in his yard during October.
Steve Turner

▼25057's very last revenue trip took place on Friday 13th March into North Wales with the Anglesey Aluminium–Llandudno Junction trip freight, seen here passing Penmaenmawr. Although moved to Vic Berry's Leicester scrapyard within weeks for disposal, it did in fact survive for preservation on the nearby Great Central Railway.   *Larry Goddard*

▲Pairs of Class 25s made the Cambrian line all their own with popular haulage of summer passenger trains, and the very last example to visit the route was No. 25191 on Tuesday 17th March, two days after the withdrawal deadline, with the civil engineer's inspection saloon from Crewe to Aberystwyth, and photographed at Trewern near Welshpool. Regarded as one of the best of the fleet, it was sold with 25278 to the North Yorkshire Moors Railway for record prices of well into five figures. *Geoff Bannister*

▼Renumbered in 1985 to indicate their reportedly superior condition, the twelve Class 25/9s in fact lasted no longer than the rest of the class. No. 25904, may have been the last to reach the Western Region on 17th March with a Berkeley Power station (Gloucester) nuclear flask train and was withdrawn three days later. It was later bought for preservation after a trip to Vic Berry at Leicester for inspection and asbestos removal. Although destined for the Severn Valley Railway, it was still on BR property on 27th December, parked at Tyseley depot awaiting transfer. It is to regain its old number of D 7633. *Paul Biggs*

▲Unlike BR policy of the past, the long lines of withdrawn Class 25s at Crewe only lasted a few weeks because sales were hurriedly arranged with one scrap dealer, Vic Berry of Leicester. The input also included some long withdrawn examples from Swindon Works which could not be cut up there by the time it closed. This one, being finally dismantled on 17th November, had been out of traffic since December 1982.
Paul Biggs

▼The only Class 25 "locomotives" left running on BR are two of the former Scottish Region electric heating units. No. 97252, pictured at Stratford-on-Avon on 11th October, has been painted in InterCity livery to match the charter stock it is normally attached to when working of Marylebone, while 97251 (BR's last Beyer Peacock built loco) was actually withdrawn at Carlisle during November, but reinstated after repairs. The third, 97250, was relieved of its Derby Carriage Works test role during October and condemned.
Bert Wynn

▲It could never have been planned for a Class 24 to outlive its Class 25 successor, but Derby RTC did not finally condemn its 1960-vintage test train loco until 4th December, not least because its replacement was written off during the summer with fire damage. No. 97201's demise was hastened by lack of spares, crew knowledge, and vacuum-brake only status. It had been removed from capital stock as No. 24061 as long ago as August 1975. Does preservation await? It was a visitor to Coalville open day on 31st May.   *John Tuffs*

▼A locomotive type which disappeared quietly from the scene at the end of December was Class 82. The withdrawal of Euston-Stonebridge Park ECS loco No. 82008 to comply with the asbestos deadline also ended British main line railways 140-year association with products from the Beyer Peacock factory at Gorton, Manchester. 82008, the penultimate loco of its type delivered in November 1961, had with sister 82005, also withdrawn during the year, outlived the rest of the class by over five years.   *Brian Morrison*

▲Although many had undergone extremely costly refurbishment only two years previously, BR decreed it wanted rid of the entire Class 27 fleet by the middle of July. With a couple of exceptions, it succeeded. A hitherto unheard-of desire to stage a rapid clean-up of Scottish depots saw most of them tripped to Vic Berry's Leicester scrapyard within days of being switched off, but there was sufficient interest for six to pass into preservation. This is a Scottish scene now sadly gone – 27059 drifts through Burntisland on a engineers ballast train on 23rd April.
Les Nixon

◄6th July was axe day for most of the Class 27s, but four, Nos. 27001/5/8/66 were retained because of lack of other motive power. No. 27066, highest numbered, is pictured on PW duty at Kilwinning on 14th July, and it survived another fifteen days to become the second last in traffic. Last of all was No. 27008, retired on 18th August. Since then, Nos. 27001/5/8/50/66 have drifted into preservation.
Bert Wynn

▲By way of a contrast to the picture on the preceding page, this picture shows that BR had certainly not extracted every last drop of energy from its Class 27s. The same 27059 was repainted by Eastfield depot and moved south from Scotland under its own power on 23rd August to Tyseley depot, where further attention enabled it to make appearances at open days including Basingstoke on the Southern Region. It was used to haul trains during the Severn Valley Railway's October diesel weekend on 10/11th October, and was even organised to haul a railtour from Birmingham to Chester via Derby and Manchester until it was called off at very short notice on the orders of an InterCity manager. Its future was still undecided at the year end. It is seen at Bewdley with NS (formerly Manchester–Sheffield Class EM2) 1500 V d.c. electric loco 1502 (27000) *ELECTRA* on 11th October. *Stephen Widdowson*

▼One of the biggest, most curious, and saddening events of 1987 was this pile of locomotive bodies at Vic Berry's Leicester scrapyard. It made national newspapers, regional TV, and at least one book cover. Reason for it was that Berry's could not cope with the midsummer influx of locos they had bought, so simply removed the bogies and power units, and stacked the shells to save space, and then cut up at leisure. Is your favourite loco here? This sideways view on 20th September shows, top row from left, 27049/ 23, 25095 (obscured), 27017/26/02, 25180/164/260/ 193, 27004, 25324/323, centre row 27053/25, 25249, 27208/055, 25288/134/327/306, 25906/154/196/ 212/042, bottom row 27037/41, 25199, 27063/45, 25058/161/034/207/093/126/ 192/902/230/089. *Information Kevin Howard/Photo Steven Knight*

BREL Doncaster ended its association with Class 50s at the start of the year as repairs were handed over to their home depots, Laira and Old Oak Common. Last loco tripped north to Doncaster, where all 50 have been maintained and refurbished since 1977, was No. 50019 *Ramillies* on 27th January. Its NSE livery looked somewhat out of place in the windswept Cambridgeshire wastes of March depot on 11th January, halted for several days because of brake problems (and a defective power unit).

Howard Johnston

Class 50 No. 50049 *Defiance*, the last loco built for BR by English Electric at Vulcan Foundry, started 1987 as just an ordinary workaday loco, and ended it as one of the Western Region's greatest enthusiast attractions. The reason was its selection for conversion into a freight loco with refurbished bogies, and regeared traction motors to give greater haulage potential at lower speed. In its old guise, 50049 nears Winchfield with the 0817 Exeter–Waterloo on 31st May.
◄ *Alex Dasi-Sutton*

▼Transformed externally by the new Railfreight livery, *Defiance*, renumbered 50149 to suit, took to the rails again on 24th September after rebuilding at Laira. Sunday 18th October saw it undertake three runs up the incline between Westbury and Warminster, stopping and restarting with increasing loads. It is pictured on the final run of the day, in pouring rain, lifting 22 loaded PGA stone hoppers, total weight 1122 tonnes, up the 1 in 75 past Dilton Marsh Halt. Future conversions have not been authorised, not least because of the cost of reinstating sanding gear removed at refurbishment, and 50149 has been relegated to a role as a Class 37 stand-in on Cornwall china clay workings.

Geoff Gillham

▲The long-threatened first Class 50 withdrawal took place on 24th February, and the choice was No. 50011 *Centurion* because of its high accumulation of TOPS hours. It worked the 1S15 12.15 Penzance–Glasgow parcels from Plymouth to Crewe, and then entered works for use as a mobile test bank for overhauled 2700 h.p. EE power units prior to their despatch to Laira. It is seen in this role on 5th June.

Colin Marsden

▼ Although F exams continued at Laira, two more Class 50s were withdrawn for spares. No. 50006 *Neptune*, the first to visit Doncaster for refurbishment back in 1979, was officially laid aside on 20th July to ease a critical spares shortage, after several weeks out of use with main generator trouble. Next to go was No. 50014 *Warspite*, pictured at Laira minus nameplates on 4th December, and condemned ten days later.

Colin Marsden

▲Class 73s assumed a temporary top-link role on the stopgap Waterloo–Weymouth service when Class 432 4 Rep units were withdrawn to allow traction motors to be transferred to new Class 442 stock. Here, No. 73131 in the interim and increasingly rare revised blue paint style, is seen with a 4 TCB set west of Hook on the 07.41 Poole–Waterloo on 26th September. *Michael Collins*

▼The all-blue Class 73 disappeared quietly from the SR scene during May as the last one, No. 73121 *Croydon 1883–1983* entered works for intermediate overhaul. Before that in the queue for attention and repainting into the standard InterCity livery was No. 73128, seen at Battledown flyover on 2nd March with the 06.36 Willesden–Southampton Speedlink. *David Warwick*

▲A blind eye was quietly turned to BR's livery policy to enable Stewarts Lane staff to repaint Class 73 electro-diesel No. 73004 in the appropriate shade of all-over NSE blue for its naming *Bluebell Railway* by TV celebrity Johnny Morris at a ceremony at newly-electrified East Grinstead on 19th September. The Bluebell, incidentally, proudly boasts it has remained diesel-less.

Howard Johnston.

▼During their last months in service the class 25 locomotives found deployment on Civil Engineers' trains. On Sunday 8th February No. 25288 heads the 7L08 Whitmore (Staffs.) to Mold Junction ballast train at Holywell Junction. The locomotive will propell its train back into the yard at Mold Junction.

David Rapson.

▲While other BR sectors chose radically new liveries for their locomotives and rolling stock, Parcels sat on the fence, and restricted itself to a simple broad red and yellow stripe on a single Class 08 shunter based in Manchester. Several ex-passenger DMUs and CCT vans also received this paintstyle. No. 08721, also unofficially named *STARLET*, is seen at Manchester Victoria on 25th April.

John Augustson.

▼The London and North Western Railway is poorly represented amongst preserved steam locomotives, and the Crewe Heritage Festival was a good enough excuse for the local depot's Class 08 shunter No. 08907 to be painted in lined black with cast cabside numberplate. Less obvious is that the loco was built in 1962 at Horwich, the works of the long-time rival but later LMS companion Lancashire and Yorkshire Railway! Location, Basford Hall yard. Date, 13th September.

David Rapson.

▲A line-up of eight redundant 204 h.p. Class 03 shunters made a melancholy sight at the 30th May Norwich Crown Point open day. The locos, widely used on empty coaching stock and lightly-laid dock lines throughout East Anglia since 1958, have been displaced at their last Norwich, Ipswich and Colchester outposts by track improvements and a more plentiful supply of dual-braked Class 08s. Gateshead followed suit at the end of the year, leaving Birkenhead as the last user on BR of this once numerous class. Pictured are, from the right, Nos. 03112, 03084, 03399, 03197, 03397, 03189, 03158, and 03089.

Iain Scotchman

▼Never a headline maker, but 1952-built 165 h.p. Ruston and Hornsby shunter No. 97650 was the oldest diesel locomotive in BR stock until withdrawn from Reading depot on 22nd April. Perhaps better known as PWM 650 (a number it retained to the end), it was one of a fleet of five built specifically for the Western Region's civil engineer, and three still survive. Honour of being the oldest loco has now passed to Bletchley's Class 08 veteran 08011. Date of the photograph is 11th October.

Michael Collins

◄The only Sulzer-engined BR locomotives of which none were being withdrawn were the veteran 33-strong 1160 h.p. Class 26s, whose duties became more diverse as they took over many workings in Scotland from the later-built but less successful Class 27. Before they could be fully utilised however, many had to visit works for removal of asbestos from their cabs, and in the event Crewe was eventually chosen for the work. This was the works yard on 31st October, with 26014 and Railfreight-liveried 26010 awaiting treatment.

Brian Morrison

▼Faced with spiralling repair costs from power unit problems and a host of minor accidents, the Southern Region started the full-scale rundown of its Sulzer-engined BRCW Class 33 fleet with 14 withdrawals up to the year end. Locos from other regions and new-build multiple units have taken over their duties. Members of all three sub-classes were casualties, including the first 33/2s. One of them, No. 33210 (withdrawn 5th August), passes Mitcham Junction on 7th February with a football special to Norwood Junction conveying Manchester United supporters to the first division match against Charlton at Selhurst Park.

Chris Wilson

▲A policy change midway through 1987 suddenly turned English Electric Class 20s from useful locomotives to an expendable commodity. Thus major overhauls ceased and withdrawals were demanded if repairs exceeded low cash limits. Even so, they still had to take over from Class 25s on LMR workings from the end of March, and this meant breaking new ground. Such was the case with the Stanlow–Aberystwyth Shell oil tank train, seen heading through Dovey Junction behind Nos. 20124 and 20151 with the return working on 29th July. Since this photo, Class 37/4s have become involved with this working.

Andrew Bannister

▶Class 20s became a regular sight in the North East as Thornaby depot's allocation increased to 14 to handle Boulby potash traffic from the Saltburn line, and other activities north of the Tees. One such working was tank traffic over the Seal Sands branch where single class 20s were ideal with their view both ways out of one cab because of the reversals on the route from the main line at Billingham Junction. No. 20076 was in charge of the 6P01 Tees Yard trip on 15th July.

Michael Rhodes

▶And this is where the money ran out. Although far from life-expired, plans to mothball mechanically defective members of the 20129–228 Series 2 fleet at March and Haymarket depots pending repair were reversed at the year end. Several were towed to Doncaster for power unit and bogie recovery, and the remains taken by lorry to Vic Berry's Leicester scrapyard for dismantling. 20191, built as recently as February 1967, was in the yard on 17th November along with 1966-built Nos. 20155/62.

Paul Biggs

◄Twenty-four Brush-design Class 47s fell by the wayside during 1987 as BR created a hit-list of run-down Class 47/0s, early-design Class 47/4s, and imposed severe cash limits on accident repairs. Even so, heavy overhauls on the 476 survivors continued unabated at Crewe, Doncaster, Springburn, and Stratford. The final five ETH, twin-tank conversions were completed, and new workings were established as other loco types declined even faster. As for prototype No. D 1500, now 47401 *North Eastern*, it was as busy as ever, attached to the Trans-Pennine Provincial Services fleet. Here, it takes a Newcastle–Liverpool service out of Northallerton on 24th August.

Les Nixon

▼As liveries became more and more diverse, No. 47522 was adorned with a unique scheme akin to LNER Apple Green for naming *Doncaster Enterprise* at the new Level Five depot's open day on 3rd October. The Parcels bodyside logo, since removed, was still in place when it was in charge of the 15.44 Manchester departure at Edinburgh on 31st October.

Bert Wynn

▲The livery scheme for non-freight owned Class 47/4s continued to be blue during 1987, complete with yellow wrapped round the cab ends, full-length large BR logo on the bodysides, and large numbers – except No. 47513 *Severn*, which was outshopped with small number transfers. It is seen leaving Southampton on 25th July with the 08.56 Cardiff–Weymouth.   *Alex Dasi-Sutton*

▼Stratford's Class 47 used to have few workings outside East Anglia... until electrification rendered many of them surplus. Some of the famous "Counties" went to the Western Region, and this one, Network SouthEast liveried No. 47582 *County of Norfolk*, now the property of Old Oak Common, is distinctly out of place on the 10.30 Aberdeen–Plymouth, pausing for signals south of Alnmouth on Sunday 6th September.   *Steve Miller*

▲This was how 1987 ended (and 1988 started) for BR's most famous non-preserved loco, green-liveried 1958 English Electric Class 40 doyen No. D 200 – working freight turns. Transfer from Carlisle Kingmoor, its home for four years, to Crewe from 4th October heralded a season of workings such as ballast trains to Penmaenmawr on the North Wales coast. It was pictured under the loading facilities there on 12th November.

Larry Goddard

◀There were some passenger turns however for D 200 in its last full year on BR, including a couple of spells rostered on the 05.15 Holyhead–Cardiff and the 13.00 return working. It was on this latter duty at Sandycroft near Chester on 31st July, but poor advertising meant that patronage was a fraction of its potential. *David Rapson*

◀D 200 reached the South Coast at the end of September as one of the working stars of the Basingstoke Rail Week. The 26th and 27th saw the 'Green Goddess' run a shuttle from Basingstoke to Andover to link up with steam specials over the Ludgershall branch, but the final run involved a capacity-loaded round trip taking in Salisbury, Southampton, and return via the Romsey loop.

David Warwick

▲Although the ranks of Class 40s workable or otherwise were severely depleted during 1987, one that did come back to life was split-headcode survivor No. 40135. Not only that, it was lovingly restored to 1960s green livery like No. D 200, and after exhibition at Tyseley open day during October was actually used to haul passenger trains again on the Severn Valley Railway. The year had started badly however, as the loco, a very shabby departmental 97406, was en its way to Swindon Works for breaking up, but was halted at Gloucester and sent back north. It has also been exhibited at Hereford and Didcot. Formal preservation now awaits this lucky veteran. Photographed at Tyseley before repainting, 18th August.   *Melville T. Holley*

▼No apologies for another photo from Vic Berry's scrapyard at Leicester, which was very much a focal point for enthusiasts' attention during 1987. Preservation attempts failed for No. 40001, and after its disposal at Swindon, other Class 40s including former MOD loco 40046 and LMR exhibition loco 40063 were towed north for breaking up. Here are their asbestos-lined remains stacked in the yard on 4th July.   *Howard Johnston*

▲The attractive colour scheme attached to Derby Technical Centre's Brush Class 31 loco No. 97203 hides the severe fire damage which caused its withdrawal in April before it could even be fully commissioned to replace veteran Class 24 loco No. 97201 *Experiment*. 97203, the former 31298, is pictured dumped at Bescot on 24th October.   *Gavin Morrison*

▼Enter 97204. Derby RTC quickly picked up a replacement for fire-damaged 97203 in the shape of 31326, which was in Doncaster Works at the time for attention to minor collision damage. The loco, which as D 5861 was the penultimate member of the class built at Loughborough in October 1962, had not been repainted in RTC colours by the year end. It is seen at Crewe on 29th October with Park Royal DMU 975089/90 in tow.   *David Rapson*

▲The end of the extensive British Coal rail complex at Ashington in March was sudden, and demolition men moved in within days to clear the site. The last BR train had in fact run on 22nd December 1986, although a handful of Class 14s soldiered on for a few weeks. Amongst them was Swindon-built No 506, ex-D 9504, pictured on 20th January. Its fate, and the rest of the fleet, is listed elsewhere in this book.   *Michael Rhodes*

►What are three BR Class 07s doing on the Waterloo–Exeter main line? They are in truth Ministry of Defence 1961-built Ruston and Hornsby 0–6–0 diesel-hydraulics which were working from the now-closed Central Ammunition Depot at Bramley near Basingstoke to their new home at the Central Vehicle Depot at Ludgershall on 2nd March. The trio, Army Nos 435, 420 and 421 are seen nearing a siding at Overton to await the passing of the 10.10 Waterloo-Salisbury. With them are former SR bogie brake vans ADS 56286/99.   *David Warwick*

COACHING STOCK

31st December 1987 marked the important deadline for the withdrawal of all asbestos-contaminated passenger rolling stock on BR, but the unreliability of replacements forced trade unions to agree to an extension. Even so, vast numbers of first generation DMUs and pre-1965 hauled coaches were taken out of traffic as new builds, electrification and changing traffic patterns took their own individual tolls.

LOCOMOTIVE-HAULED STOCK

Provincial Services has declared disinterest in inheriting other sectors' cast-offs, and together with loss of many of its own loco-hauled services promises the scrapping of large numbers of Mark 2 design vehicles. 1987 witnessed the first inroads into the ranks of vacuum-braked Mark 2 TSOs and BSOs, and a few 1968-build air-braked and dual heat Mark 2a and 1969 Mark 2c were withdrawn for departmental conversion or export. Mark 1s were inevitably heavily attacked in all sections, although many of the later batches have some life left in them in dedicated use such as Paddington and Great Eastern suburban, and InterCity charters and excursion stock.

The only type rendered extinct was the NVX, or two-tier car van built by Newton Chambers in 1961–62 with glass-fibre bodies. The last five ended their days on the East Coast Main Line.

One humorous unrenumbering took place during 1987 when high security letter mail vans 80460–3 were returned to their original BG identities to avoid their presence in a train being an easy giveaway to potential train robbers!

There was no totally new hauled stock delivered during 1987. The conversion of the former HST TRFKs into modular catering vehicles for the West Coast Main Line was completed, and a start made, on the similar hauled RFBs in the 10000 number series. In Scotland, withdrawn Class 101 trailer 54356 officially became coach 6300, classified OC, after conversion into an observation saloon for the Inverness–Kyle of Lochalsh route.

Network South East started the refurbishment of its Mark 2 vacuum-braked stock used on the Liverpool Street–King's Lynn service. The first TSO emerged from Eastleigh Works in December fitted with new APT-style seats. The toilets were also tarted up.

DIESEL MULTIPLE UNITS

The orders of lightweight Class 142s and 144 Pacer units were completed early in the year, although many of the former ended up in store with a multitude of gearbox and wheel defects. Of the more hardy Sprinters, 1987 saw the delivery from BREL York of the entire series of 85 gangwayed Class 150/2 two-car units. Nine of the Class 155 variety were also delivered from Leyland, although most needed instant surgery for body problems. Metro-Cammell also managed the first of its 114 Class 156 units.

Big inroads were made into older classes, including the last of the Cravens Class 105s in normal service. Swindon-built Class 120s borrowed by Scotland were also heavy casualties, along with West Midlands and South Wales Derby Class 116s, and a number of both Gloucester Class 119s and BRCW Calder Valley Class 110s. Even the trusty old Metro Cammell Class 101s started to succumb in sizeable numbers.

On the Southern, the advent of the East Grinstead line electrification enabled the withdrawal of the 20 worst Class 204, 205, 206 and 207 units, leaving just two Class 203 units as the sole survivors of the old narrow-bodied Hastings line stock.

ELECTRIC MULTIPLE UNITS

The inauguration of the Peterborough, Cambridge and East Grinstead electric services together with a general increase in Network SouthEast business more than soaked up any excess rolling stock, so the stock situation barely changed during 1987. Only newcomers on the a.c. front were the first ten class 319 units ready for the 1988 'Thameslink' service, while on the third rail the first of the new Bournemouth line stock emerged from BREL Derby before the year end.

Withdrawal was restricted to a dozen of the more venerable Class 415 4 EPB units, Class 414 2 Haps, and Class 416 2 EPBs. Service reductions cost the lives of four Isle of Wight cars. After some indecision, all the former North Tyneside 62xx units were condemned, but many have entered departmental service instead.

The Great Eastern and LM a.c. fleets remained virtually static, while Scotland admitted to the withdrawal of two asbestos 1967-build Cravens Class 311 units only after they had been consigned to the scrap merchant.

LIVERIES:

After the general chaos of the previous transitional year, serious attempts were made to marshall complete rakes of stock in the new sector liveries of InterCity, NSE and Provincial, although the still large numbers of blue and grey vehicles were widely apparent. The much-criticised NSE "toothpaste" livery was toned down somewhat, and the stripes at the end of the bodysides of EMUs curved to give a better appearance. Class 411s continued to receive the now obsolete "Jaffa Cake" paint style of brown and beige with broad orange stripe. InterCity stuck to its guns, the only modification being the addition of the sector legend in the new typeface, and much smaller bodyside numbers.

Provincial adopted the style of the Trans-Pennine blue and beige for its new DMUs as well, and good old fashioned blue and grey for everyone else except the West Highland Line, which got a new rake of LNER-style green and cream Mark 1s with steam haulage in prospect. The distictive Sealink-liveried Mark 1s of red, white and blue were all withdrawn, however. Somewhat incongruously, the former West of England brown and cream Class 142 Pacers went straight into service in Leeds and Manchester in their same colours.

It seemed everyone had to have a green unit for special occasions. Newest additions to the fleet were the four-car Class 203 Hastings line gauge 203 001, and Great Eastern Lines Class 302 four-car set 302 207.

▲Down the...
ham...
serv...
som...
of...
star...
ansv...
and...
its...
tion...
115...
fron...
Uni...

▲Three of the original Class 150 Sprinter vehicles were refitted with 2 + 2 seating and air-conditioning, and re-geared for 90 m.p.h. travel as a sample of future "delights" of Provincial travel. Reclassified 154 001, DMSL 55201 and DMS 55401, formerly 150 002, were delivered from Derby at the beginning of the year, and the centre trailer followed many months later. They were on a Derby–Birmingham New Street service on 28th December. *Dennis Taylor*

▶A...
thei...
whe...
ago...
the...
disg...
550...
Lei...
und...
550...
the...
aw...

▶If the three-car Class 154 Sprinter was planned, the three-car Class 150 certainly wasn't! To meet pre-5th October South Wales timetable commitments, new stock sent from Neville Hill to Cardiff was temporarily reformed. Here, 150 274 joined to DMSL 52270 stand at Canton fuelling point before working a Valleys service on 9th September. *Barry Nicolle*

▶T...
sho...
arr...
wa...
els...
lar...
two...
an...
Sw...
W...
res...
53...
tio...
se...
ai...
m...

▶The biggest Sprinter series yet will be the 23-metre Metro-Cammell Class 156, which although a novelty at the end of 1987 will eventually number 114 two-car units nationwide. Initial deliveries were slow however, and only a couple had been delivered by the year end. 156 401 made its first trial runs from Washwood Heath works to Banbury on 10th November, and is pictured here on the 13th passing Leamington. *Chris Morrison*

▲One of the smartest-ever EMUs showed itself just before the close of 1987 and inspired the BREL Derby Carriage Works workforce to believe they had something to be proud of. Twenty-four five-car 100 m.p.h. Class 442 units have been ordered for the Waterloo–Bournemouth service, which will be extended to Weymouth from May 1988. Costing £1.5 million apiece, they seem to have successfully overcome the visual problem of the end gangway. Special features include a return to compartment accommodation for first class, a guard's van in the buffet vehicle, plug doors, and on the economy side', reused Class 432 4 Rep traction motors. Note the combined bodyside unit and coach number.   *BREL*

◄Into the 1990s, this is how the new Class 465 Networker promised to North Kent commuters might look. With no end gangways (at this stage), it will replace early post-war slam-door 4 EPBs. The mock-up was at Derby on 14th December.   *Colin Marsden*

►BREL also outshopped the first of its four-car Class 319 Thameslink Class 319 EMUs in early autumn. Unit No. 319 002, pictured inside the inspection shed at Selhurst on 14th November, was formally accepted by NSE director Chris Green at a ceremony on 2nd September 319 001, used for trials at Strawberry Hill, nosed its way into the reconstructed Snow Hill tunnel for the first time on 22nd October, but only got a few feet before blowing a fuse. Anticipation of a big demand for the through-London service (Bedford–St Pancras patronage is up 50 per cent in four years) saw the order for the £75 million order increased in May from 46 units to 60.

David Brown

▲Only those with a good brain could keep track of all the reformations of Bournemouth line stock during 1987 to enable some Class 432 4 Reps to be withdrawn for traction motor removal for installation in the new Class 442 power cars. Only two original units, 2007/14 remained by the end of December, and with the use of Class 438 4 TC trailers the rest had gone through the Class 492/8 (4 TCB, Class 438 trailers with TFK replaced by Class 432 TRB for Class 73 loco haulage) and Class 432/9 (Class 432 minus one power car) phases. This photo takes a last look at the time-honoured formations that have been with us since the end of steam in 1967 – 4 Rep No. 2005 and 4 TC No. 8012 are propelled by Class 33/1 33102 across Farlingham Junction on 28th February with the 1032 Weymouth–Bournemouth–Waterloo fast service. The location is where the non-electrified line from Fareham joins the Portsmouth mainline, and on this date Weymouth services were being re-routed via Guildford, Havant, Fareham and St. Denys because of engineering work at Worting Junction, west of Basingstoke.   *David Brown*

▼The Eastern Region took delivery of cascaded LMR Class 310 stock, but it remained physically unchanged. Not so the domestic Class 302s however, as a handful lost their trailer second vehicle and swapped power cars. The front end renumbering is somewhat crude on 302 439 (formerly 302 239), arriving at Wickford on 18th August with the 1737 Liverpool Street–Southend.   *Iain Scotchman*

▲The East Coast Main Line HST fleet completed a staggering two million miles per unit during 1987, an achievement completed in nine years compared with nearly twice that time for the Deltics they replaced. BR admits that they are however at least half way to being life-expired, and one eye was focussed on the future when power car 43123 was equipped with Time Division Multiplex equipment at Derby RTC for use as a driving trailer for push-pull trials with special stock and a Class 86 loco out of Euston. One of the first test trains is seen behind No. 86240 *Bishop Eric Treacy* at Rugby on 20th November.   *Bert Wynn*

▼The quartet of Mirrlees-engined HST power cars Nos. 43167–70 all entered regular service during 1987 on Western Region domestic services, to favourable responses from engineers and operators. The last conversion No. 43170 is seen returning to the WR from Derby Works through Burton-on-Trent on 21st May with ex-works stock but no rear power car.   *John Tuffs*

▲Although there were no wholly new coaches for BR during 1987, there were many important conversions to update main line fleets. Derby Carriage Works was busy creating RSMs (Restaurant Buffet Modular) from HST TRFKs, and hauled RFBs and FOs. No. 10224, formerly 11062 and intended for the West Coast Main Line fleet, carries the new InterCity paint style at Derby on 18th September. *John Tuffs*

▼Ten spare SLE Mark 3 sleepers have been overhauled at Derby for lease to Danish State Railways for use on the Copenhagen–Esbjerg route. They have been given the DSB dark blue and red livery. *BREL*

▲The Scottish Region found an alternative to exhausting historic observation vehicles on the scenic Inverness–Kyle of Lochalsh route by converting spare Metro-Cammell Class 101 DMU trailer No. 54356. Partitions were removed, carpets, random seating, and public address installed, as well as loco-compatible ETH. Livery is normal, except for loss of the full yellow end. The coach, renumbered 6300, made its debut on May 21, and is seen at Garve on the 1005 to Kyle on 15th July with loco 37262 *Dounreay* at the head.　　　*Paul Biggs*

▼Also in Scotland, the West Highland Line got a fresh set of Mark 1s for steam specials, this time dual heat instead of just steam, which were repainted in the LNER tourist livery of green and cream. At the end of the year, Polmadie handed over responsibility for the set to Bounds Green, with some interesting unscheduled suburban workings as a result. Most outstanding was a run to Peterborough behind a Class 86 loco. BCK No. 21241 is pictured at Fort William on 31st August.　　　*Tom Noble*

DEPARTMENTAL:

Departmental numbers TDB 977486–ADB 977567 ere allocated in 1987, these numbers encompassing a ixture of sandite coaches, instruction coaches, test ain coaches, laboratory coaches, S & T stores vans d even a DSU DP 13 Chemical Carrier Unit! It is rhaps not surprising that Unit 026 (ADB 977559/60) is ing referred to as a Carriage Cleaning Fluid Unit as pposed to its official name! Amongst other vehicles ken into the departmental coaching stock fleet were ass 101 Metro-Cammell power cars 51433, 53167 and 3246 which have become DB 977391–3 respectively, ose departmental numbers having been reserved in 86. DB 977391–3 were stripped of asbestos at Vic

Berry, Leicester in June 1987 and sent to Cardiff Cathays where they are being converted to ultrasonic test train coaches.

Of those departmental coaches or vans condemned or scrapped in 1987, DW 28804 attracted the most interest. DW 28804 was formerly Mink W 28804W, built as long ago as 1906, and active for 81 years, latterly as a RCE staff and dormitory van for Crane DRP 81520. Following minor internal damage sustained after a rough shunt, DW 28804 was condemned and almost immediately sold to Woodham, Barry Dock for scrap as a result of a 'spot' sale. Fortunately this sale was subsequently cancelled and DW 28804 is to be offered for sale through the Director of Supply at Derby.

Built in 1906 DW 28804 was finally withawn from its latter departmental role as a CE staff and dormitory van following dame sustained in a shunting incident. It was otographed at Radyr marshalling yard on h October. *Deryck W. Lewis*

A historic vehicle which disappeared without oper recognition was one of the 1957 series Mark 1 revised prototypes built by Cravens Sheffield. Open First W 3082 featured a ndow design without ventilators that was pied in the "blue pullman" vehicles. It entred departmental service in 1973 as DB 975278, used by Derby Technical Centre Laboratory Coach 15, a mock-up for the PT catering vehicle. It is seen at Vic Berry's eicester scrapyard on 1st May. *Paul Biggs*

TECHNOLOGY

Four important technological applications affected BR in 1987. Firstly, solid state interlocking of signals was used in a number of resignalling schemes. This been mentioned previously under signalling. Secondly, 'Aptis' and 'Portis' revolutionised ticket issuing. Thirdly the purchasing by BR of the new dynamic track stabilisers promised to mean an end to those week-long 20 mph speed restrictions from which passengers have suffered for so long. BR also purchased a new two-car track recording DMU.

The revolution in the issuing of tickets came about by the introduction of new computerised ticket machines both for booking office and on-train use. The idea was first developed by BR Research & Development Division at Derby, and developed commercially into the booking office version (APTIS – "All purpose ticket issuing system") and the on-train version (PORTIS - "Portable ticket issuing system"). The major benefit of both systems to BR is that accounting information is stored automatically as tickets are issued. For passengers needing to purchase tickets on the train, a major benefit was that tickets could, in theory be purchased from anywhere to anywhere. In practice, that sometimes could prove difficult.

If quantity was the only criterion, 1987 has been a relatively quiet year as regards the purchase of on-track plant by BR. Indeed, Plasser and Theurer who are the main supplier of on-track plant only supplied five machines to BR. However this order included two major new developments – the first self-propelled Dynamic Track Stabiliser and 09 CSM machines purchased by BR. Dynamic Track Stabiliser DR 72201 was allocated to the Eastern Region and was a critical element in the establishment of a speedier way of ballasting track to cut delays caused by engineering works. The old technique meant that a new section of track had to be run in by trains travelling slowly before the ballast was compacted. Temporary speed limits could last up to four weeks. With the new technique a gantry lifts a section of track, the old ballast is smoothed out and new track laid. Once the track is laid back, the ballast is laid in layers of 25 to 35 centimetres. The Dynamic Track Stabiliser has eight retractable flanged wheels slung under the centre of the machine which can be pressed down on to the rails by jacks with a total force of 32 tonnes. Smaller horizontal wheels grip the outside of the rails so that they can be vibrated laterally. One pass of the stabiliser has the same settling effect on ballast as 100,000 tonnes of normal rail traffic. It i estimated that as a result seventeen minutes can b trimmed off the London–Edinburgh journey-time, be cause less slack will be needed in the timetable to allow for route maintenance. Projected savings on that rout alone are a £1,000 a day in brake wear and a furthe £600 in fuel.

1987 also saw the arrival of 09-CSM machines on BR with the arrival on the Eastern Region of 09-16CSM DR 73001 and 09-32CSM DR 73101. Unlike convention al tamping machines the tamping heads are no mounted on the machine itself, but carried on a sub frame with its own wheels for guidance and partia support. The 09-CSM moves forward at a constan pace, only the tamping sub-frame is accelerated an decelerated within each tamping cycle. As conventiona tampers have to be accelerated and braked sharpl within each working cycle, the 09-CSM saves not onl energy but reduces mechanical stresses on the machin as a whole. As a result of the success of the DTS an 09-CSM an order for DR 72202–13 and DR 73102– was placed with Plasser and Theurer at the end of 1987

Also worthy of mention was the purchase in 1987 o Permaquip DX 98401 an underground line work site DX 98401 is not meant to carry personnel other tha the operator and is equipped with manually operate hoists and jibs for loading purposes. DX 98401 is use on the Waterloo and City Line and since its arrival i October 1987 is often to be seen on the surface stable outside Waterloo Station.

Almost all departmental coaches are conversions fro capital stock vehicles. However in 1987 a two-coac purpose built departmental was taken into stock class fied as class 180/1. The body shell of the two-coac track recording unit was built at York, whilst th recording and analysis system for the new unit wa designed by BR Research and constructed by Vistech o Belper and Geoquip of Wirksworth. DB 999600 is th instrumentation coach, whilst DB 999601 is the accom modation coach. DB 999600/1 will be used on cross country and local routes all over Britain.

► Portis Ticket

≥ British Rail

From
DORE ✳   OUT
To
SHEFFIELD ✳   ⇌
Route

Class   Adults
2ND CHILD NIL
Ticket Type   Children
CHEAPDY RTN CD ONE
Price   Date
£0.20M 18.FBY.87

6691 6295 E 21.43
Number
7728 6690669100000
Valid
AS ADVERTISED
Tear ticket along perforation

Valid Off Peak as Advertised

Class   Ticket type   Price

Valid on   Number

Between   Valid

Route/also available at

valid within R zone(s) indicated

≥ One Day Capitalcard ⊖   ◄ Aptis Ticket

▲Two new track machines that arrived from Plasser and Theurer during the year are seen together passing Leicester Holding Sidings on 9th June. DR 72201 is a Dynamic Track Stabiliser whilst DR 73001 is classed as a 09-16CSM Tamper/Liner. Both had recently arrived in the country when the photograph was taken.   *Paul Biggs*

►Undergoing final testing at Permaquip's test track on 1st October is DX 98401, a maintenance vehicle for use on the underground Waterloo and City line.   *Permaquip*

▲Spare London Underground 1973 stock trailer No. 514, which had never been in passenger service, was converted at BREL Derby to TRC666, the conversion being completed in May 1987. Technically the vehicle performs the same track recording functions for London Underground as British Rails DB 999550 and mechanically it is coaching stock compatible (standard buckeye coupling, e.t.h. and control cabling for Southern Region working). Since, on occasions, this vehicle may be required to work over the BR system jointly with DB 999550 a BR departmental number has also been allocated. The photograph shows DB 999666 at Norwich Crown Point open day on 30th May 1987. *Dennis Taylor*

▼En-route from Vic Berrys, Leicester to Cardiff Cathays workshops on 16th June were DB 977391/2/3. Vic Berrys had undertaken asbestos removal from the vehicles which will be converted to a new ultrasonic test train. The three vehicles are pictured as part of a freight train at Abbotswood Junction.

Stephen Widdowson

▲Purpose-built Track Recording Unit DB 966000/ DB 96601 stands in the yard at the Railway Technical Centre, Derby on 5th November undergoing final fitting out of instrumentation.   *Colin Marsden*

▶The instrumentation and control unit inside DB 999600.   *Brian Morrison*

BR MISCELLANY

ALMOST GONE

▲If you have a green unit there will always be special work for it! It was somewhat appropriate that green class 105 Cravens unit Nos. 53359/54122 should be used on the last day of DMU service on the Hitchin–Huntingdon–Peterborough service. With Class 101 power–trailer set 51185/54352 in tow it is seen at Sandy with the 19.20 Hitchin–Peterborough service on 10th May.
Mick Burgoyne

▼Both the unrefurbished class 37 locomotives and clay hood wagons were on "borrowed time" in the West Country as refurbished class 37/5s were allocated to Laira depot during the year replacing the unrefurbished allocation. Replacement of the clay hoods by modified MGR wagons was due to be effected during 1988. 37196 *Tre Pol and Pen* was photographed at St. Blazey whilst working a Goonbarrow–Lostwithiel service on 24th April. Shortly afterwards 37196 was denamed and transferred to Inverness.
Mike Goodfield

SEVERE WEATHER

▲1987 was a notable year for freak weather – snow, storms and floods, with lives lost on BR as a result.

SNOW.

▲The Southern Region actually suffered worse from the cold than the better-prepared Scottish, and the blizzards of 11/12th January meant Inverness's Beilhack self-propelled snowblower had to be sent for to clear the tracks in North Kent. Snow was up to platform level in places, but commuters still complained about cancelled trains! It took until 18th January for services to return to normal. This was an unusually deserted Surbiton on 14th January, when de-icing unit No. 008 made a special run to clear more overnight snow.

Colin Marsden

▼Not that it was much warmed up the East Coast either.... HST power car No. 43080 soldiers on despite the cold as it brings up the rear of a London-bound service leaving Alnmouth on 14th January.

Stephen Miller

SPECIAL SERVICES

▲A special Birmingham–Ironbridge tourist service was introduced on 19th July to serve the heritage museum. The local council is actively supporting the Sunday service, not least as a way of reducing acute traffic congestion in the area. The 14.08 Ironbridge Power Station Sidings–Wolverhampton crosses the famous Albert Edward Bridge over the River Severn. There are outline plans are for a Victorian-style station at Ironbridge.

Geoff Bannister

▼A Class 205 DEMU made a nostalgic return to the Mid-Hants line from Alton on 20th September as part of the preserved line's 10th anniversary celebrations. 205 006, which might have visited the line in BR days in its old guise as 1106, approaches Ropley.

Hugh Ballantyne

▲Three important milestones in English Electric locomotive development are seen together at Basingstoke Open Day on 27th September which brought together the greatest ever gathering of BR motive power, past and present. Class 40 prototype D 200/40122 is pictured on a special Andover shuttle, accelerating past green-painted Class 20 pairing 20030 + 20064 and Class 55 Deltic 9019 *ROYAL HIGHLAND FUSILIER.*
    Howard Johnston.

►The 30th anniversary of the Hastings DEMUs was celebrated with the re-painting at Eastleigh in July of the re-formed four-car Class 203 unit 203 001 in green livery. On 26th September, it was at Uck-field, a station soon to be transformed by track re-modelling, with the 12.42 service to Charing Cross.
    Les Nixon.

◄The Severn Valley Railway attracted large crowds of modern traction enthusiasts twice during the year as it attracted visiting modern motive power to haul specials at its diesel weekends. Here, Class 44 'Peak' D 4 *GREAT GABLE* arrives at Arley with maroon Mark 1 stock.
Colin Underhill.

▼Seventeen years out of synchronisation. Bewdley station lost its BR services on 5th January 1970, yet was visited by a Class 150 Sprinter DMU on 9th May 1987 as part of the Severn Valley Railway's diesel weekend. Unit 150 143 has steam for company.
Stephen Widdowson.

▲The Class 20 Locomotive Society's 'Three to the Sea' railtour from Sheffield to Brighton on 2nd May was enhanced by the use of Nos. 20064 *'River Sheaf'* and 20030 *'River Rother'*, which were painted green specially by Tinsley depot staff. By contrast, the threesome was made up by 20118 in Railfreight grey, and the ensemble is pictured passing Crystal Palace.   *David Brown*

▼Class 20s are also rare on the Central Wales Line, but Pathfinder Railtours took Nos. 20021 and 20113 there on 21st July with a 'Welsh Rambler' tour from Leicester to Gloucester. They are seen heading north through Craven Arms.   *Andrew Bannister*

▲The last time a pair of Class 27s worked down the East Coast Main Line was on 14th March when a Scottish Railway Preservation Society farewell railtour was organised from Falkirk to Newcastle and Carlisle. The objective of raising funds to buy an example was achieved, but not with either of these two, 27046 and 27049, which went for scrap. The SRPS bought 27005 instead. The picture location is Heaton.

Les Nixon

▼'The Dunstabelle', the first passenger train to traverse the Luton–Dunstable branch for 22 years, took locals to Brighton on 3rd May. It was organised by ADAPT, An action group campaigning for regular services on the line. The stock employed was Class 33/1 push-pull loco 33119 and 4 TC unit 8019.

Kevin Lane

Two named Class 33s visited the Midland Main Line together on 31st May for the occasion of the annual Coalville open day. No. 33027 *Earl Mountbatten of Burma* and 33056 *The Burma Star* are seen near the top of Bagworth bank on the Leicester–Burton-on-Trent line in charge of the Hertfordshire Railtours 'Coalville Scrutator' tour from London St. Pancras. Butterley was the ultimate destination. *John Tuffs*

A Class 50 worked through Barnsley on 14th October with the 'Skipton Skipper' railtour from Bristol. 50020 *Revenge* takes the Barnsley branch off the main line at Wincobank Station Junction. *Les Nixon*

▲The supply of Peaks ran so short as to make Class 45 double-headings rare towards the end of 1987, although the Pathfinder railtour from Bristol to Scarborough and Hull on 3rd October employed one of both types. The station buildings at Malton form the backdrop for 45107 and 45007.

Les Nixon

▼On 24th April the "Friends of the National Railway Museum" chartered the departmental 'York Saloon' for a tour of collieries in the Nottinghamshire, Derbyshire and South Yorkshire coalfields. The train is seen at Clipstone South Junction with Clipstone Colliery visible to the right.

Les Nixon

▶DEMU 203 001 winds its way over the Weymouth Quay branch on 8th August with the 'Hastings Diesel Swansong railtour'. Starting at Charing Cross, it also visited Reading, Newbury, Frome, Whatley Quarry, and Castle Cary.
Alex Dasi-Sutton

▼St Leonards traction maintenance depot at Hastings closed its doors on 3rd October, but only after a number of ceremonies to commemorate the staff's efforts in maintaining the area's DEMU and loco fleet for the last 30 years. Power car 60014 of green-liveried four-car Class 203 unit 203 001 was named *St Leonards* on 11th September, and the following day the unit was used on a staff excursion to Bournemouth and Weymouth, pictured passing Preston Park, Brighton.
Rodney Lissenden

LOOKING AHEAD

All of the regions where LRT is proposed launched major publicity campaigns with extensive use made of glossy colourful brochures.

All of these brochures showed the environmental benefits that light rail systems will bring to the areas, and were illustrated with artists impressions showing the light rail vehicles in the particular City context.

▶Illustration of brochure issued in March in connection with the Greater Manchester PTE scheme.

▼West Midlands PTE have adopted the "Midland Metro" name for their proposed system. Livery is basically white with black/blue/green lining and logo.

▲ As part of a demonstration for Manchester's light rail system, a Docklands car was loaned and exhibited at Debdale Park, Manchester. Docklands car No. 11 was fitted with a pantograph and is pictured at the official inauguration on 10th March.
Les Nixon

street level with a low floor running nearly 18 metres in the centre and raised areas at the ends over the motored bogies. Plans are well advanced for extensions of this truly modern system.

In Nantes studies for further extensions were announced during the year and in Paris the Bobigny LRT line is under construction. Proposals during 1987 have indicated that LRT is being considered seriously in Brest, Rennes, Rouen and Toulouse. These new systems when constructed, together with the existing ones in Lille, Marseilles and St Etienne will cement the future of LRT in France.

The question of disabled accessibility is now being considered very seriously and various studies were

under way during the year. New low-floor cars in service or at construction stage in Bremen, Genève and Würzburg as well as Grenoble mentioned above, and an extensive study was taking place under the directorship of the West German Association of Public Transport Operators (VOV).

As will be seen from this short account, Light Rail Transit is very much to the fore in public transport planning and operation and with its proven ability to attract ridership, help reduce motor traffic, pollution and noise, and be a cornerstone in the rejuvenation of our inner cities, the future of Light Rail Transit in Europe and the UK is, happily, very promising.

DOCKLANDS LIGHT RAILWAY OPENS

▲The Docklands Light Railway linking Statford and Tower Gateway with Island Gardens in the East end of London was officially opened in August. The service is provided by six-axle articulated cars as typified by this example near Heron's Quay on 24th November. Whilst the Docklands Light Railway origins lie within the mass development of the east end docks it has become evident that the existence of the railway itself is now creating further development of the area and making it an attractive proposition for companies to relocate offices.

Alex Dasi-Sutton

▼Tower Gateway station is at the London end of the Docklands Light Rail system. On 3rd September unit No. 10 waits with a service bound for Island Gardens. In the background can be seen British Rail's Fenchurch Street station. *Hugh Ballantyne*

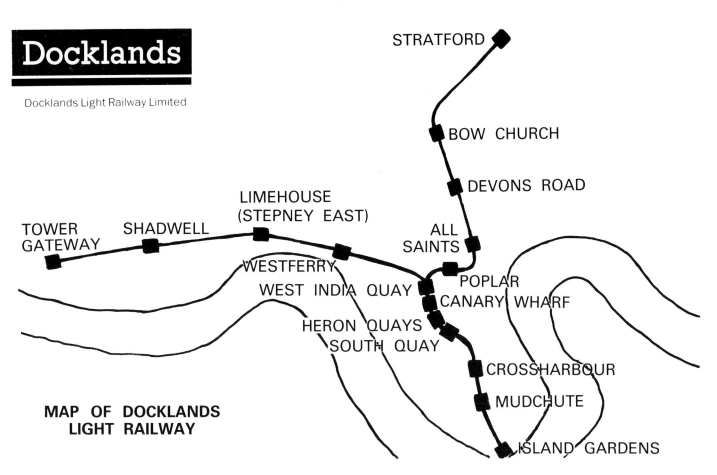

Docklands

Docklands Light Railway Limited

STRATFORD

BOW CHURCH

DEVONS ROAD

LIMEHOUSE
(STEPNEY EAST)

TOWER
GATEWAY

SHADWELL

ALL
SAINTS

WESTFERRY

POPLAR

WEST INDIA QUAY

CANARY WHARF

HERON QUAYS

SOUTH QUAY

CROSSHARBOUR

MUDCHUTE

**MAP OF DOCKLANDS
LIGHT RAILWAY**

ISLAND GARDENS

▼An interior view of car No. 11, showing the Duewag-type articulation over the centre bogie typical of virtually all modern European light rail vehicles. All cars feature driverless operation by means of computer control.

Hugh Ballantyne

PRESERVATION

Preservation of the past is one of Britain's fastest-growing industries, and the railway movement certainly seems to be playing its part.

Headlines of 1987 were the inauguration of the East Lancs Railway, providing Manchester with its own tourist line; unabated expansion plans by other railway centres; large-scale purchase and return to service of important steam and modern traction exhibits; the LNWR 150th anniversary celebrations and the imposition of admission charges at the National Railway Museum.

There was rejoicing at Bury Bolton Street station, a 1950s period piece, on 25th July when the first four miles of the East Lancashire Railway scheme were opened, to Ramsbottom. The project, using existing track which last carried passengers to Rawtenstall 15 years earlier, had taken seven years to bring to fruition, and up to £1 million local authority cash. It was however instantly promoted straight into the big league, collected the 1987 ARPS main award, and carried over 10,000 passengers in its first eight days of operation.

For steam enthusiasts, the line's immediate Achilles heel was the lack of ex-BR main line steam power, although an array of large diesels brought enthusiasts of a different kind.

Elsewhere in the UK, existing schemes also made good progress.....

The Great Central Railway made inroads on its three-mile southern extension from Rothley to Birstall (Leicester).

The Peak Railway obtained permission to lay its first quarter of a mile of track at Darley Dale, two miles north of Matlock.

The Gloucestershire and Warwickshire succeeded in reaching Winchcombe on 2nd August, two and a half miles from its Toddington base.

The North Norfolk Railway marked the centenary of the first train to Holt in 1887 by running the first train since closure by BR in 1964 over the two and a quarter miles from Weybourne.

The Llangollen Railway pressed ahead with its plans to extend to Corwen.

The Isle of Wight Steam Railway was given a major shot in the arm by BR's offer to help finance the restoration of the three and a half mile section to reconnect with BR at Smallbrook Junction.

The Yorkshire Dales Railway won permission to extend from Embsay to Draughton, closer to its eventual Bolton Abbey target.

On the Welsh narrow gauge, 1987 looked as it would be the last for the Vale of Rheidol Railway under BR ownership, when continuing losses prompted talk of a sale.

MUSEUMS:

Crewe celebrated the 150th anniversary of the founding of the London and North Western Railway in fine style. First came an open day at the BREL works,

◄The HST coach in the background is the giveaway, but one of the events of the year nonetheless was the visit of Gresley A4 4–6–2 4498 *SIR NIGEL GRESLEY* to King's Cross in the early hours of 31st May en route from the Norwich open day to Marylebone. The 50 min stay was the first appearance of an A4 at King's Cross since the farewell tour in 1964. *David Percival*

▲The North Norfolk Railway completed its two and a quarter mile southern extension from Weybourne to Holt for the first diesel passenger trains on July 18. The new section, closed in 1964, was in fact inaugurated by GER J15 0–6–0 564 on June 16, but needs considerable track work before it can return during 1988. The first train to use the extension was an engineer's weedkilling special on 22nd April. *Brian Fisher*

▼Later in the year a railbus service was introduced which travelled to within 100 yards of the new station site at Holt. One of the Waggon und Maschinenbau railbuses preserved on the North Norfolk railway is seen on this service on 30th August.

Brian Fisher

▲Big event in the world of preserved lines was the reopening of the first section of the East Lancashire Railway from Bury to Ramsbottom on 25th July. Fifteen years after passenger services ceased, Greater Manchester Council has backed the scheme which will eventually cover eight miles to Rawtenstall. The inaugural services were hauled by ex-Manchester Ship Canal Hudswell Clarke 0–6–0T No 32 *Gothenburg*, double-heading Meaford Power Station RSH No. 1. Eight trains each way are scheduled during the summer months. The photograph shows the inaugural train departing from Bury Bolton Street.

Richard Fox

▼Peak Rail's ambition of restoring passenger services over the former Midland route to Buxton made a small step forward during 1987 with the laying of the first section of track at Darley Dale. After access was given to the site, clearance of scrub preceded the laying of sleepers during October. The site, pictured on 6th November, will initially be used to store materials.

Brian Cuttell

►Preservation of a different kind.... the six old Pullman Company cars at Marazion, Cornwall have been bought by a local hotel owner for modernisation as holiday homes. In this 7th September view, rare 1914 BRCW six-wheeler *MIMOSA* is in the foreground awaiting renovation. Others on the site are Alicante (1914) and Calais (1921/3) vehicles *AURORA*, *FLORA* and *JUNO*.

Stephen Widdowson

followed by a cavalcade of steam and diesel locomotives from the new Heritage Centre which brought The Queen face to face with LMS 4–6–2 PRINCESS ELIZABETH named after her 54 years earlier.

Birmingham Railway Museum meanwhile cast its eyes on the freshly redundant 1906 GWR Moor Street terminus as perfect for steam tours over the three miles to its Tyseley base.

Steam returned to Swindon Works during November with the creation of a Heritage Centre and workshop, although the first two occupants were ex-SR Bullied Pacifics 34072 257 SQUADRON and 35027 PORT LINE.

Beamish Open Museum in the North East was named as European Museum of the Year 1987.

From April 6, it cost £1.50 for adults to visit the hitherto free National Railway Museum. The charges reflected a change in Government policy.

STEAM LOCOMOTIVES:

Undoubted highlight on the steam scene was the return to the UK in April of ex-LSWR M7 0–4–4T 30053 after 20 years in the United States. It was destined for the Swanage Railway.

Not far behind in importance was March's decision by the Bluebell Railway to construct a new LB&SCR Marsh "Atlantic" using a virtually identical Ivatt Great Northern-design boiler recovered from a factory in Essex. The loco could however take up to 20 years to complete.

LNER A4 Pacific steam record holder 4468 MALLARD made a few trips out on the main line, and GWR King 4–6–0 6000 KING GEORGE V marked its 60th year and perhaps last on the main line with a farewell run on 26th September upon expiry of its boiler certificate.

The trend of loaning locomotives produced some unfamiliar, often remarkable sights, not GWR Prairie 2–6–2T 5572 on the Keighley and Worth Valley Railway.

Congratulations are extended to those who returned ex-Barry wrecks to steam: 5080 DEFIANT (GWS Didcot), 7822 FOXCOTE MANOR (Llangollen Railway), 7828 ODNEY MANOR (Gloucestershire and Warwickshire Railway), 30506 (Mid-Hants Railway), 34027 TAW VALLEY (Severn Valley Railway), 34105 SWANAGE (Mid-Hants Railway), 47279 (Keighley and Worth Valley Railway), 48151 (Midland Railway Centre), 53808 (West Somerset Railway), and 80080 (Midland Railway Centre).

In the meantime, the prospect of every loco still at Barry being saved improved with the sale of no less than 10 to the Cardiff Bute Road museum, and five more to the Pontypool and Blaenavon Railway.

Steam was active on the main line, and on some new routes. The Cambrian Coast Main Line featured 7819 HINTON MANOR, 46443, and 75069. An LNER-design 2–6–0 returned to the West Highland Line's Mallaig extension after a 25-year absence with the appearance of Class K1 2005, while LMS 5305 "ALDERMAN A.E. DRAPER" was employed on the southern section from Fort William to Craigendoran. LMS Jubilee 5593 KOLHAPUR worked between Chinley and Buxton, S&D 53809 between Andover and Ludgershall, and 35028 CLAN LINE, 53809 and 75069 on Nottingham–Derby–Matlock workings.

DIESEL & ELECTRIC:

The change in BR traffic patterns was reflected in a record number of diesels moving into preservation, helped by a lifting of the ban on sale of asbestos-contaminated locomotives, which had the offending material removed by contractors as part of the deal.

Important locomotives saved were pre-war LMS shunter 7069 from France, the sole-surviving Andrew Barclay Class 06 shunter 06003; prototype Class 08 shunter D 3000; large numbers of Class 25s and 27s, and the entire stock of Class 14 diesel-hydraulics rendered redundant at British Coal Ashington, including first-built

D 9500, and last-built D 9555, also the final BR locomotive constructed at Swindon Works back in 1965.

The National Railway Museum also decided to lay claim to an entire rake of the ill-fated Advanced Passenger Train stock.

There seemed still no prospect of BR lifting its ban on the use of preserved diesels to haul trains, although Class 40 loco D 200 enjoyed its last full year in traffic on a variety of special workings. Other withdrawn but BR-owned locos, including Class 27 27059 and Class 40 D 335 (97406/ 40135) were actually restored to preservation condition, and used on private lines.

STEEL LOCOMOTIVES PRESERVED FROM BARRY:

No.	Moved to	Date
2859	Llangollen	30/10/87
2874	Blaenavon	20/08/87
3855	Blaenavon	13/08/87
4253	Blaenavon	18/08/87
5538	Llangollen	31/01/87
5668	Blaenavon	13/08/87
5967	Blaenavon	12/08/87
30830	Bluebell Railway	28/09/87
45163	Humberside LPG	12/01/87
76077	Toddington	08/05/87

◀Year by year, the GW Manor 2–6–0s rescued from Barry scrapyard return to steam. 1987 saw two of them, 7822 *FOXCOTE MANOR* (illustrated), and 7828 *ODNEY MANOR* exiled from the Gloucestershire and Warwickshire Railway. 7822, still in undercoat, was part rebuilt at Oswestry before moving to the Llangollen Railway for completion. It is seen there on 17th December making its first outing to Berwyn.
Bert Wynn

▼After a few worries on the way, including the fitting of a replacement boiler, LSWR Urie S15 4–6–0 506 was restored to traffic on the Mid-Hants Railway on August 26. The loco, the 79th rescued from Barry scrapyard in April 1976 after a twelve-year stay there, has been restored to Southern Railway livery, and carries the boiler from Maunsell-design 30825. It is pictured partnering Bulleid 4–6–2 34105 *SWANAGE*, also on its rededication day, at Chowton on the climb up to Alton.
Hugh Ballantyne

▲An LNER design 2–6–0 returns to the West Highland Line after a 30-year absence. The North Eastern Locomotive Preservation Group's Thompson Class K1 No. 2005 coasts through Fassfern between Fort William and Mallaig on 27th August. *Les Nixon.*

▶Two ex-Barry locomotives which returned to steam within days of each other also worked over BR lines to attend the October Ripple Lane open day. BR Standard Class 4MT 2–6–4T 80080 and Stanier LMS Class 8F 2–8–0 48151 are seen near Pye Bridge en route from the Midland Railway Centre at Butterley to London. *Brian Cuttell.*

▲In BR days, Great Western Manor 4–6–0 7819 *HINTON MANOR* was for a long time kept in spotless condition to work the Cambrian Coast Express, so it was appropriate that this veteran should be around again when 1987 steam specials were organised west of Machynlleth with the help of the Severn Valley Railway. Strong local goodwill resulted in heavy loadings. 7819 is pictured rounding the coast at Penhelig with the 13.40 Machynlleth–Barmouth on 27th May.   *Les Nixon.*

▼The Buckinghamshire Railway Centre was generous to the Mid-Hants Railway in lending its Metropolitan Railway Class E 0–4–4T No 1 for the 10th anniversary gala weekend. It is pictured in full steam at Ropley on 20th September.   *Hugh Ballantyne.*

▲The Tay Bridge centenary was marked on 20th June by a steam shuttle over the famous structure. Locomotive chosen was a LNER V2 2–6–2 No. 4771 *GREEN ARROW*, a type well-known to the area until 1967. GREEN ARROW worked five coaches from Dundee to Wormit, where it was caught by the camera in a familiar location.   *Les Nixon.*

▼The Vale of Rheidol Railway made the headlines twice during 1987. BR announced on 18th November it was looking to sell its sole remaining steam line, although the rules mean a formal closure notice will have to be issued first. Secondly, even the reign of steam is threatened by the arrival of a 150 hp Baguley 0–6–0 diesel-mechanical loco ordered for a Mozambique sugar plantation but never delivered, in an attempt to slash annual fuel bills. It has been given the number 10. The Aberystwyth–Devil's Bridge narrow gauge line carried an estimated 50 000 passengers during 1987. Will this scene soon change? Pictured is the line's original locomotive No 9 *PRINCE OF WALES* passing Rhiwfrow on 3rdOctober.   *Andrew Bannister.*

▲February marked the tenth anniversary of the end of Class 52 Westerns on BR as well as mainline diesel-hydraulic operation on BR. 1987 was however a good year for the class, with most of the seven preserved examples in the public eye. After extensive repairs and repainting, the Western Locomotive Association's D 1062 *WESTERN COURIER* has stock to match its maroon livery as it hauls a Kidderminster–Bridgnorth train past Northwood Lane at the Severn Valley Railway's gala day on 11th October.   *Keith Lawton.*

▼The Beyer-Peacock Class 35 diesel-hydraulic B–B design was 25 years old, but only four of the 101 examples built have survived from the mass withdrawals of 1971–75. Oldest survivor, the Diesel and Electric Group's D 7017 (pictured here), worked a Hymek Silver Jubilee tour over the West Somerset Railway on 26th September, while sister D 7018 was an exhibit at both Basingstoke and Tyseley, and D 7076's rebuild at Bury reached the repainting stage.   *Howard Johnston.*

▲Surely one of the most remarkable sights ever on the Keighley and Worth Valley Railway must have been Churchward Prairie tank 5572, which left its Great Western haunts for a month to attempt the Yorkshire banks between Keighley and Oxenhope. The loco, part of the GW Society collection at Didcot, is reported to have shown a keen dislike for Chesterfield coal, repeatedly requiring unscheduled stops for a "blow up". It was pictured near Haworth on 12th April with a mixture of Mark 1 suburban and open stock. *Rodney Lissenden*

▼The Llangollen Railway has still a long way to go with the restoration of its ex-NCB Great Western pannier tank 7754, but sister loco 7715 showed what is to come when it spent from 14th July to 20th September on loan from the Buckinghamshire Railway Centre. This loco, originally sold out of service to London Transport, accelerates out of Llangollen station for the line's current terminus at Berwyn. *Brian Dobbs*

▲Two operational Bullied West Country light Pacifics side by side, a sight not seen since the end of steam on the Southern in July 1967, was re-created at Ropley on the Mid-Hants Railway on 26th August. The occasion was the completion of the nine-year restoration of unrebuilt 34105 *SWANAGE*, which is pictured leaving the shed to make its first official run. On the left is an earlier ex-Barry restoration job, rebuilt version 34016 *BODMIN*.

Hugh Ballantyne

▼The ambitious scheme to build a Brighton LB&SCR Marsh Atlantic from virtual scratch got under way at the end of March with the decision to buy a similar Ivatt boiler discovered during 1986 at a factory in Essex. The project may take 20 years to complete, and the boiler is seen at Sheffield Park on 19th September.

Howard Johnston

▲Drummond LSWR M7 0–4–4T 30053 returned to British soil on 6th April after 20 years in America. The 14-day sea crossing ended at Felixstowe Docks, and the loco, bought by the Southern Repatriation Group for £24,000, was put on exhibition at Swanage station prior to a full restoration to working order.

Andrew P M Wright

▼Easter Sunday 19th April's gala day on the Great Central Railway offered super power for one of the line's eight-coach rakes. The 16.20 Rothley–Loughborough featured both recently-restored BR Standard Class 8P 4–6–2 71000 *DUKE OF GLOUCESTER* and the one of the locos which displaced it from top link West Coast Main Line duties back in 1962 – English Electric Class 40 No. 40106 *"ATLANTIC CONVEYOR"*. The double-header is seen coasting near Woodthorpe.

John Gosling

▲For steam, two former Somerset and Dorset Joint Railway 2–8–0s stole the limelight, and justifiably so. Here, the well-travelled 53809 is rounding the curve out of Bridgnorth with the 14.20 service to Kidderminster as part of the Severn Valley Railway's gala day on 10th October. It was on loan from the Midland Railway Trust at Butterley.
Hugh Ballantyne

▼The S&D closed in 1966, and 53809 returned to almost within a stone's throw in October when specials were run from Andover to Ludgershall as part of the Basingstoke Rail Week celebrations. It also produced the strange, and hitherto unique culture clash of a Fowler-design 2–8–0 hauling strictly 1980s-livery Network South East coaching stock! This shot shows it passing Red Post, near Andover, with the first leg of the final steam working on 27th October.
Geoff Gillham

▲The other surviving S&DJR 7F 2–8–0 53808 was brought back into life after 23 steamless years on 15th August after restoration by the West Somerset Railway's own engineers. The loco has generated a substantial contribution to the railway's record fare receipts during 1987. It is pictured leaving Williton with a ten-coach special to Bishops Lydeard on 19th September.   *David Wilcock*

▼There could have been no more appropriate exhibit at the bicentenary celebrations at the Ministry of Defence camp at Long Marston than LMS Stanier 8F 2–8–0 No. 8233, which survived active service in the Middle East during the Second World War and is now dedicated to railwaymen who lost their lives during the conflict. It ran under its own steam from the Severn Valley Railway via Worcester to take part in the event of 3rd and 4th October which also featured a demonstration freight over the five-mile branch to Honeybourne. Hunslet 0–6–0ST Royal Engineer was also on display.   *Stephen Widdowson*

▲1987 marked the end for the time being, of the main line career of Great Western King Class 4–6–0 6000 *KING GEORGE V* upon expiry of its seven-year boiler certificate. Hauling authentic maroon stock to match its own post-1957 livery, the 60-year-old Swindon loco has just passed the west end of Severn Tunnel Junction yard on the return leg of the 'Severn–Wye Express' from Hereford to Newport, Gloucester, Swindon, Gloucester, and back to Newport. The following week's diamond jubilee trip was halted by a derailment in Gloucester Yard, and the final run of all was from Swindon to Newport and Hereford on 26th September.
Melville T. Holley

◀Another GW Castle 4–6–0 returned to steam, but Birmingham Railway Museum's 5080 *DEFIANT* suffered hot box troubles and missed its planned main line debut on the 5/6th September's 'Carmarthen Express' between Swansea and Carmarthen. The loco, which was also named *OGMORE CASTLE* during its career, is pictured at Walton-on-Trent, returning from weighing at Derby on 9th September.
Bert Wynn

▲Although people turned out in their thousands for the special charity walk through the tunnel to the new Birmingham Snow Hill station, they sadly did very little on 26th September when BR took the trouble to provide GWR Castle 4–6–0 No. 7029 *CLUN CASTLE*for the very last passenger train out of the old Moor Street terminus, the 21.05 to Dorridge, returning to Tyseley. The £10 a head special attracted little support, but still made a memorable sight with wreath on the smokebox door.   *Melville T. Holley*

▼Modified Hall 4–6–0 No. 6990 *WITHERSLACK HALL* was a major contribution to the Great Central Railway's operational fleet when it became fully operational during the early part of the year after an 11 years complete rebuild from a Barry wreck. The loco, pictured on the 16.45 Loughborough–Rothley at Woodthorpe on the GCR's Easter Sunday 19th April gala day, has never been a stranger to the route because it took part in the 1948 Locomotive exchange trials which took it from Marylebone to Manchester via Sheffield and the old Woodhead Tunnel.   *John Gosling*

▲The first steam-hauled train over the West Highland Line for 25 years took place on 17th October courtesy of immaculately turned out LMS Black 5 4–6–0 No. 5305 *"ALDERMAN A.E. DRAPER"*, and all 344 seats were sold out within ten days of being put on sale. 5305, itself 19 years into preservation since BR dropped its fire at Lostock Hall at the end of steam, is seen at Bridge of Orchy on the return trip destined for the southern limit of Craigendoran.   *Les Nixon*

▼LMS Jubilee 4–6–0 No. 5593 *KOLHAPUR* returned to the Settle and Carlisle line on 19th March after a gap of 20 years with a 'Cumbrian Mountain Express' railtour, and happily without incident. Another run called the 'Mancunian' was also made on 18th April, and the loco is seen near Barons Wood.   *Hugh Ballantyne*

▲'Lizzie and Ethel'... The addition of a Class 25 ETH generator between steam loco and stock is now an essential feature of many specials, although actively despised by recordist and photographer alike. This does not detract however from the spectacular smoke effects created by BR's heaviest mainline runner, LMS Princess Royal 4–6–2 6201 *PRINCESS ELIZABETH* as it leaves Skipton on 7th February with its first southbound trip over the Settle and Carlisle route, and at 13 coaches its heaviest since BR days.   *Gavin Morrison*

▼By contrast, the tiny features of the Ivatt Class 2MT 2–6–0 are dwarfed by the mountains and scenery of the Cambrian Coast Line as the Severn Valley Railway's 46443 ambles between Fairbourne and Tonfanau on Sunday 5th August with the return Cardigan Bay Express from Pwllheli to Machynlleth. Although essentially the summer's standby loco, 46443 was the most regularly used of the three available.
Andrew Bannister

▲A dump of steam locomotives in a military camp deep in forests in Central Finland. All are now to be scrapped or sold, as the reserve fleet is to be disbanded. A 2–8–2 No. Tr1 1067 leads the line up of 20 locos on 13th June.   *Brian Garvin*

▼Finnish Railways (VR) DMU trailer painted in a trial new livery. Note the "EXPRESS" logo.   *Brian Garvin*

▲The new Amsterdam–Brussels 'Benelux' push-pull sets went into full service in 1987. One of these sets is seen at Rotterdam C.S. with Dutch Plan ICR-Bs driving trailer second No. 50 84 28-70 103-3 leading and Belgian Railways No. 1181 (not visible) propelling the 10.26 Amsterdan C.S.–Brussel Zuid service. *David Brown.*

▼Regular TGV services between Paris and the Côte d'Azur started in April 1987. Set 05 *RIS-ORANGIS* is seen at Nice Ville on 9th April 1987 with an e.c.s. working. *David Brown.*

ÖBB 150th ANNIVERSARY

▲The ÖBB anniversary parade was held at Strasshof, north of Wien on three weekends. Gölsdorf 2–6–4 310.23 makes a fine sight as it steams past the many spectators on the 13th September with a train of vintage passenger stock. *Peter Fox.*

▼The latest class of locomotive in the ÖBB fleet is the Class 1146, actually a rebuild for dual voltage working from the Class 1046 motor luggage vans. 1146 001-1 is seen in the same parade with a freight train. *Peter Fox.*

„Die Parade der Bahn"

Bahnhof Strasshof

150 JAHRE EISENBAHN IN ÖSTERREICH

▲Austrian private railways also took part in the anniversary parades. Here GySEV No. 17, an 0–6–0 built in 1885 is seen hauling a goods train. *Peter Fox*

▼An aeriel view of the exhibition held at Wien Nord with (left to right), new overhead line units, a new DB Class 628.2 DMU, 2180.01 and MAV V60 036. *Brian Garvin*

WEST GERMANY

1987 was dominated by the delivery of the class 120 electric locos and their teething troubles. The first loco was delivered at the beginning of the year but by the year end there were few in regular traffic which gave an extra lease of life to the class 194s. However the new DMUs of class 628.2 seem to have been introduced without any great problems.

Construction of the high speed lines continued with some stretches expected to open in 1988. The production batch of ICE EMUs was authorised with 40 sets featuring in the order.

On the negative side more branch lines were closed and freight services rationalised allowing many diesel locos of class 260/1, 322/3/4 to be withdrawn. Late in the year DB reclassified its class 260/1 shunting locomotives to shunting tractors, being renumbered to classes 360/1, thus allowing drivers establishments to be reduced. Another saving in this area came from the decision to fit radio controls to some shunting locomotives so that they could be driven remotely by shunting staff.

ITALY

Vast amounts of money were injected into FS and all sections of the railway reflect this. New locos, carriages, wagons, track renewals, electrification, can be seen from one end of the system to the other. At the same time plans have been drawn up for the closure of many lightly used lines which brought with them strike action by railway personel.

The class E632, E633 electric locos continued to be delivered as were the last examples of the order for D445 diesel locos. No new DMUs were delivered as the intended closures will release many units. FS received towards the end of the year the first of its new high speed trains – the class ETR 450 EMU and after tests the first units were expected to enter service in early 1988.

LUXEMBOURG

1987 was a quiet period as electrification works slowly moved forward from Luxembourg towards Gouvy.

THE NETHERLANDS

One of the major changes for the year has already been mentioned under Belgium – the revamp of the Brussels to Amsterdam services. Another major development was the opening of the first section of the Flevolijn to Almere and with it some new stations.

New 3-car EMUs for Inter City services continued to be delivered allowing older plan E loco-hauled stock to be withdrawn. However the new diesel locos of class 6400 were delayed but this did not halt the continuing withdrawal of class 2400 diesel locos.

NORWAY

A period of consolidation for NSB. New tilting main line carriages were delivered which allowed improvements on the Trondheim route to take place which were matched by the introduction of further class E117 electric locos. Some second hand diesel shunters were obtained from West Germany allowing worn out examples to be withdrawn.

PORTUGAL

Another system that managed to take a hard look at itself and started to draw up plans for future spurred on by EEC membership. All branch lines were reviewed and some closures expected. The big Alsthom diesels of class 1900 seem to be less than successful as visitors to Barreiro always found many out of use. On the Porto–Lisboa route the electric loco fleet was augmented by further deliveries of class 2600 from Alsthom/Sorefame whilst passengers benefited from the new coaches based on SNCF Corail stock. These were also introduced on the principal services from Barreiro to the Algarve. Plans were drawn up for the road bridge over the Tagus from Lisboa to have railway tracks added.

SPAIN

Having previously had a spate of closures RENFE announced its plans for the future in a programme that includes new lines, carriages, and locomotives. One of these plans got the green light almost immediately – the high speed line from Madrid to Andalucia with work due to start by the year end. Whilst some of the trains for this new line may be EMU it is also envisaged that high speed loco-hauled services will be needed.

A new station was also announced for Sevilla. This will be at Santa Justa and will replace the existing terminals at Plaza de Armas and San Bernado. Over the last 10–15 years RENFE has pursued a policy of rationalising termini in cities which had more than one terminal. It is quite possible that Plaza de Armas station may become a regional railway museum.

Towards the end of the year RENFE took delivery of a new batch of diesel shunters of class 309, otherwise the traction scene was rather quiet.

SWEDEN

SJ continued to receive deliveries of class Rc6 electric locomotives which meant less work for the old Du2 rod driven electric locos which were virtually out of work by the year end. The Stockholm and Malmö areas received new EMUs of class X10 for local services. No major trains service alterations took place but improvements to passenger accommodation were made by more new carriages going into service. No major service changes are expected until the new X2 high speed EMUs are introduced.

A decision was reached to modernise the oldest locos still in service – the electric shunting locos of class Ub. These were sent to Notviken Works for refurbishing and will receive equipment for them to be controlled by radio.

A new train ferry service to Denmark was introduced when operations started between Göteborg and Frederikshavn.

Towards the end of the year there was a serious accident at Lerum near Göteborg when two expresses collided head on. This was put down to S & T staff wrongly wiring points and the signalman not testing the equipment before signalling the trains.

SWITZERLAND

Operations on the SBB seem to have been affected by the railway industry's involvement in the order for electric locos for China as deliveries of the new EMUs were delayed and the SBB had to hire locos and stock from other lines for its timetable change in the summer. Some class 194 electric locos were hired from the DB and various locos and EMUs from private lines were given duties over the SBB.

Meanwhile plans were drawn up for the SBB and Switzerland's future needs with the Bahn 2000 proposals. In this scheme various proposals were made to fit the Swiss railway network for the needs of the next century.

Finally towards the end of the year the SBB took delivery of the first main line diesel locomotive for many years. This was a refurbished DB class 220 intended for use on works trains and for hauling main line services over stretches of line where the catenary has to be isolated.

▼Certain DB Class 260s and 261s were modified for remote control use. 261 237-2 is seen shunting at Ingolstadt station. Note the special hydraulic coupling arm. *Brian Garvin*

FROM TEE TO EC

1988 marked the end of an era in Europe with the last Trans-Europe-Express trains finishing with the start of the Summer timetable to be replaced by a new network of 'Euro-City' services. The Euro-City network features trains of both first and second class with a high standard of accommodation, unlike the TEE network which was first class only. The most famous TEE was of course the 'Rheingold' which made its last Journey on 30th May.

IZB
IHR ZUG-BEGLEITER

1. bis 30. Mai 1987

TEE 14/16
Rheingold
Basel SBB/München - Amsterdam

TEE 14/16 Rheingold

TEE **14 Basel** SBB **- Karlsruhe - Mannheim - Mainz - Bonn - Köln - Düsseldorf - Duisburg - Emmerich - Utrecht - Amsterdam**

TEE **16 München - Augsburg - Ulm - Stuttgart - Heidelberg - Darmstadt - Mainz - weiter als** TEE **14**

Basel—Amsterdam
München—Mainz
Basel Bad Bf/München—Oberhausen
Clubwagen München (TEE 16)—Mainz (TEE 14)—Emmerich

▲Netherlands Railways (NS) Plan Y-2 'Sprinter' EMU stands at Almere Buiten after arriving with the 15.35 service to from Amsterdam CS. This new line, known as the 'Flevolijn' was opened to the public in May 1987 with an extension to Lelystad to follow in 1988.   *David Brown.*

▼A view of Emmen Station (NS) on the recently-electrified branch from Zwolle. On the left 'Hondekop (dog-head)' EMU 713 waits to depart with the 15.17 fast train to Zwolle, whilst on the right a pair of 2200 class diesel-electric locos, with 2300 leading, arrive with a freight from the Almelo direction.   *David Brown*

A RAILWAY DIARY FOR 1987

JANUARY

1. FLOODS. Severe flooding in Mid-Wales continues to dislocate rail services between Machynlleth and Aberystwyth. Five Class 150 Sprinter DMUs stranded west of Dovey Junction.

1. HONOUR. Loco driver Stanley Haddaway of Tattenham Corner honoured with BEM for efforts in giving over 2000 lectures to 500 000 schoolchildren on rail safety.

3. PRESERVATION. Eviction fears for East Anglian Railway Museum as BR announces plans to sell land occupied by them next to Marks Tey–Sudbury branch. Society ownership eventually secured.

5. MISHAP. Weybridge station buildings gutted by fire.

5. INTERCITY. End of steam heat excursions as InterCity declares three Bounds Green charter sets as electric heat only.

6. HONOUR. Dumfries honoured as Best British Rail Station with unveiling of plaque.

6. PRESERVATION. Last Lambton Railway loco, ex-BR Class 11 shunter 12098, moved from coke works to North Tyneside Steam Railway site at Backworth.

8. WORKS. £9 067 000 bid by White Horse Holdings accepted or 150-acre closed Swindon Works site. Former 19 and 20 shops to be donated as a museum.

8. LOCOMOTIVES. Entry into BREL Doncaster Works of BR's last vacuum-brake only locomotive, Class 31 31271 for refurbishment and dual-braking.

8. CRIME. Frustrated rail traveller and Truro city councillor Christopher Mason convicted of obstruction after sitting on his briefcase in the middle of the track. Given conditional discharge, with £300 bill for costs.

8. LOCOMOTIVES. Birkenhead Class 03 shunter 03162 outshopped in green livery as D 2162 with plaque to commemorate now closed Birkenhead Mollington Street Depot.

9. PRESERVATION transfer - Class 08 shunter 08359 (D 3429) moved from North Staffordshire Railway at Cheddleton to Peak Railway, Buxton.

10. LOCOMOTIVES. What a place to fail - loco 37418 *An Comunn Gaidealach* arrives at Scotland's northernmost terminus Thurso with 17.35 ex-Inverness and then unable to engage reverse.

11. CLOSURE. Caersws loop closed on Cambrian line.

12. MISHAP. Southern Region services dislocated by heavy snowfalls.

12. LOCOMOTIVES. Penultimate operational Class 40 97405 (40060) is victim of frost damage at Allerton depot. Withdrawal follows, official date 9th March.

14. MISHAP. Continuing SR snow and frost chaos – Class 56 freight locos 56001/62 borrowed to haul stranded electric stock.

14. PRESERVATION. First Class 45 loco secured – 45060 (D 100) *SHERWOOD FORESTER* sold by tender from store at Toton depot.

17. MISHAP. Snow and frost forces abandonment of Cambridge electric VIP launch.

17. PRESERVATION. Inaugural run on the East Lancashire Railway from Bury to Ramsbottom after restoration of ex-Derby RTC Class 42 Warship D 832 *ONSLAUGHT*.

17. HERITAGE. BR marks 125th anniversary of the Somerset and Dorset Railway with its own railtour from Templecombe.

18. LOCOMOTIVES. Nine Eastern Region depots lose shunter allocations as part of centralisation plan – Colchester (to Norwich), Cambridge (to March), Lincoln and Shirebrook (to Doncaster), Barrow Hill (to Tinsley) Frodingham (to Immingham), Hull Botanic Gardens (to York), and Healey Mills and Knottingley (to York).

18. LOCOMOTIVES. Sub-class 86/0 extinct by arrival of 86007 at Crewe Works for overhaul. Will become 86407 after bogie modifications.

19. ELECTRIFICATION. First electric service train on the Bishops Stortford–Cambridge electrified extension is 06.15 ex-Cambridge involving 305 518 + 305 507.

19. ELECTRIFICATION. Ayrshire scheme completed with Ardrossan Harbour and Largs extensions.

19. RAILFREIGHT. Trials begin on Chessington branch with Class 37 loco 37222 and two-wagon load for new coal traffic from Didcot.

20. TECHNOLOGY. 43167, first HST power car re-equipped with Mirrlees MB190 engine runs trials from Derby Works.

25. ELECTRIFICATION. First Class 455 units traverse Farringdon–Blackfriars track under their own power.

26. NEW SERVICE. New £500,000 Cardiff Valleys service authorised with new stations at Ninian Park, Waun Gron, Faireater and Danescourt.

26. TECHNOLOGY. Cable-joining ceremony at Tollerton north of York marks completion of £3.3 million all-plastic London–Edinburgh communications link.

27. CLOSURE. Start of three-day hearing into future of Stratford–Henley-in-Arden rail link.

27. LOCOMOTIVES. Last Class 50 to be repaired at Doncaster, 50019 *Ramillies*, arrives.

29. METROS. £190 million investment in 1988 announced for London Underground by Transport Minister David Mitchell with ratepayers' contribution reduced by £55 million.

28. PRESERVATION. Class 44 Peak D 8 *PENYGHENT* leaves Strathspey Railway after six years for two-week journey to new home at Matlock.

30. TRAIN FERRY. *SPEEDLINK VANGUARD* makes last outward sailing of Harwich–Zeebrugge Sealink freight service (inaugurated 24th April 1924). BR favours Dover–Dunkerque route.

30. CLOSURE. Final run of Rowntree Mackintosh Speedlink from York to Fawdon (Newcastle) traffic transferred to road.

30. MISHAP. Singer. Class 37 37011 written off after colliding at high speed with ex-works Class 303 EMUs 303051/90 while running round its train.

30. LAND SALE. BR offers remaining trackbed next to closed Hunstanton terminus for redevelopment (closed 1969).

31. TECHNOLOGY. First runs in service of Mirrlees MB190-engined HST power car 43167 on Paddington–Bristol–Weston-super-Mare route.

31. STRIKE. West Yorkshire Road Car bus crews strike means 561 passengers for the Keighley and Worth Valley Railway, more than ten times the 1986 figure for the same day.

FEBRUARY

1. PRESERVATION. GWR 2–6–2T 5538 moved from Barry to Llangollen Railway.

2. CLOSURE. British Coal hands

133

The new Holmes Chord at Rotherham enabled a faster time between the new station at Rotherham Central and Sheffield. A two-car class 108 works a Doncaster–Sheffield service on 12th May.

Les Nixon

meanwhile is booming.

6. CROSS-CITY LINK. Approval given for £15 million spur between from Belfast Central to York Road stations by 1993.

6. NEW SERVICE. Inaugural run of Master Cutler HST Pullman with Cuisine 2000 catering vehicle.

6. NEW STOCK. Night Scotsman sleeper/reception lounge coach 6700 exhibited at Edinburgh Waverley.

7. CHANNEL TUNNEL. Major hurdle overcome when 30-day House of Lords select committee debate ends by suggesting no changes to the project.

8. CLOSURE. Royston station, Manchester, with re-open option after two years.

8. LOCOMOTIVES. Romney Hythe and Dymchurch Railway's Diamond Jubilee marked by Class 73 loco 73118 naming ceremony at Folkestone.

9. NEW SERVICE. Oxford–Bicester re-opens for passengers.

9. CLOSURE. Short spur between Brindle Heath Junction and Agecroft Junction, Manchester.

9. LOCOMOTIVES. Last Doncaster-built Class 58 loco 58050 named *Toton Traction depot*.

9. CHEATS. London Marathon runners banned from event after taking short cuts on Underground.

10. CLOSURE. Cricklewood TMD ends diesel maintenance.

11. ELECTRIFICATION. New Eastern Region services inaugurated between Liverpool Street–Norwich, Liverpool Street–Cambridge, and Kings Cross–Peterborough.

11. NEW NAME. Second Class tickets renamed Standard Class.

11. NEW SERVICE. Reintroduction of Nuneaton–Coventry passenger service after 22 years.

11. ELECTRIFICATION. Full 25 kV Kings Cross–Huntingdon–Peterborough commuter service inaugurated.

11. NEW SERVICE. Stockport–Heysham–Isle of Man boat train run revived after upgrading of track with local authority help.

11. NEW STATION. ScotRail opens Wester Hailes on the Edinburgh–Glasgow Central line.

11. NEW STATION. £2.4 million Rotherham Central opened, and closure plans announced for nearby Masborough.

11. DIVERTED. Night Scotsman sleeper train transferred from Kings Cross to Euston, along with London–Edinburgh Motorail.

11. TECHNOLOGY. New £500,000 Caerphilly resignalling project commissioned.

11. NEW SERVICE. Sunday services introduced on Styal and Glossop lines until September to assess demand.

11. CLOSURE. York Clifton carriage depot closed.

12. CHANNEL TUNNEL. Agreement reached on charges. Both BR and SNCF to pay 60% minimum usage charges to make guaranteed revenue more of an attraction for prospective shareholders.

12. NEW STATION. Hag Fold, Manchester.

13. OBITUARY. Tragic death in Spain of artist and railway author Brian Haresnape.

15. NEW STATION. Replacement £700,000 Abbey Wood buildings officially opened.

16. MISHAP. Birmingham–London services dislocated when Coventry FA Cup supporters push flagpole out of coach window and bring down overhead wires.

17. PRESERVATION. 10th birthday of the Friends of the National Railway Museum.

19. CHANNEL TUNNEL. Eleven firms (seven British) invited to tender for 40 new trains.

21. TECHNOLOGY. Opening of Strathclyde's new multi-purpose £5 million rail operations centre at Yoker with 22 stock sidings, washing plant, and accommodation for 270 drivers and guards. Hyndland and Bridgeton facilities withdrawn. The control centre replaces 17 signalboxes on a 43-station route.

21. NEW STOCK. New Kyle of Lochalsh line observation saloon is converted ex-Class 101 DMU trailer 54356.

21. NEW STOCK. First Class 150 Sprinter DMU 150 261 arrives at Cardiff Canton for crew-training.

22. RAILFREIGHT. Dudley Freightliner terminal closed, traffic diverted to Round Oak, Brierley Hill.

22. PRESERVATION. Steam returns to Cambrian Line with GWR 2–6–0 7819 *HINTON MANOR* on test run prior to summer service with BR 2–6–0 75069.

23. PRESERVATION. Great Western Society steam cavalcade starts eight-day celebration of Didcot centre's 20th anniversary.

26. LOCOMOTIVES. World convention of the Institution of Railway Signal Engineers at Glasgow prompts naming of Class 37 loco 37411 to suit.

27. RAILFREIGHT. 21 years of petroleum traffic from Cleveland marked by naming of Class 31 loco 31327 *Phillips-Imperial*.

30. OPEN DAY. Norwich Crown Point.

31. PRESERVATION. Network SouthEast Director Chris Green re-opens Wootton terminus on the Isle of Wight Steam Railway, and pledges support for restoration of link to BR's Smallbrook Junction provided others help with the £500,000 cost.

31. PRESERVATION. LNER A4 4–6–2 4498 visits Kings Cross en-route from Norwich to Marylebone. First streamlined Pacific there since 1963.

31. OPEN DAY. Coalville depot. Leicester–Burton freight line used for passenger shuttle service.

JUNE

1. PRESERVATION. LNER Class A3 4–6–2 No 4472 *FLYING SCOTSMAN* works privately chartered Tyseley–Leicester "Cromwell Pullman" for five days.

2. LOCOMOTIVES. Environmentalist complaints end dismantling of blue asbestos-contaminated locos at Thornton Yard, Fife. Remaining machines moved to Vic Berry's yard at Leicester.

2. TECHNOLOGY. £4.3million Liverpool Street–Bethnal Green re-modelling and resignalling scheme announced. Completion due April 1989.

3. TECHNOLOGY. £3million Inverness signalling centre completed with closure of five signalboxes, and control to Clachnaharry, Aviemore and Nairn. New £220,000 Inverness–Dingwall RETB signalling system announced, with closure of signalboxes at Lentran, Muir of Ord and Dingwall.

3. METROS. Tyne and Wear integrated public transport policy announced with new PTA/PTE symbol, new timetable, and anti-vandalism campaign.

5. LOCOMOTIVES. Last eleven withdrawn Class 25 locos moved from from BREL to Vic Berry, Leicester.

6. OPEN DAYS. Joint Worksop and Shirebrook exhibitions.

13. PRESERVATION. Last run of Class 55 Deltic No 55019 *ROYAL*

HIGHLAND FUSILIER over North Yorkshire Moors Railway before transfer to new home at Butterley.

15. LATE ARRIVAL. Guard of up East Anglian misses the train at Ipswich. Taxi chase to Manningtree gets him back aboard.

16. WORKS. Conversion of BREL Glasgow to Springburn Level Five maintenance depot marked by naming of loco 47637 *Springburn*.

16. PRESERVATION. North Norfolk Railway centenary enacted by GE 0–6–0 No 564 on Sheringham–Holt run, first through train since BR closure in 1964.

19. NEW SERVICE. BR Birmingham–Ironbridge Gorge Museum "Ironbridge Express" DMU is first regular passenger working for 25 years over freight branch.

20. HISTORY. Centenary of Tay Bridge, at 2 miles and 73 yards, the longest structure of its kind in Europe.

20. OPEN DAY. Aylesbury station exhibition. Exhibits include LNER A4 4–6–2 No 4498 *SIR NIGEL GRESLEY*.

21. FARES. InterCity Savers increased by 10 per cent.

21. TECHNOLOGY. Original Banavie signalbox demolished, replaced by new radio-control centre.

25. PRESERVATION. East Lancashire Railway re-opened between Bury and Ramsbottom.

27. OPEN DAY. Newport station exhibition.

28. WORKS. Official handover of closed BREL Swindon buildings to new owners White Horse Holdings.

28. PRESERVATION. First run in steam since restoration ex-Barry scrapyard of LMS 8F 2–8–0 No 48151 at Midland Railway Trust, Butterley.

29. NEW STATION. Re-opening of Conwy station (closed 1966) with £200,000 Gwynedd County Council and Welsh Office support.

29. EXHIBITION. Darlington Top Bank station exhibition, until 4th July.

29. ELECTRIFICATION. Planting of 13,000th ECML mast at Darlington station.

29. NEW STOCK. Sprinter and Pacer DMUs withdrawn from Blaenau Ffestiniog line because of wheel noise on tight curves.

30. LAND SALE. Haverhill station, closed 1967, sold to developer for £250,000.

JULY

2. CLOSURE. Rotherham Masborough notices issued.

3. PRESERVATION. Year-long ban on asbestos-contaminated locomotives

being sold lifted with deal for Class 25 25244 to go Swanage Railway from Vic Berry's yard, Leicester.

4. OPEN DAY. BREL Crewe Works.

4. PRIVATISATION. Talks start on sale of BR's narrow gauge Vale of Rheidol steam railway.

5. PRESERVATION. Steam returns to East Coast Main Line when LNER Class V2 2–6–2 4771 *GREEN ARROW* hauls Newcastle–Darlington Centenary Express.

5. NEW STATION. Halt opened at Chee Dale for summer Edale–Buxton Peak Forest line specials.

6. COACHES. Introduction of 26-seat lounge car for first class passengers on Kings Cross–Scotland sleeping car services.

7. LONDON. London Regional Transport's new track recording vehicle TRC 666 (BR DB 999666) makes first runs under own power with converted 1960 stock motors L132/3.

8. TECHNOLOGY. 43123 moved to Derby Works for modification to allow it to remotely control class time-division-multiplex fitted electric locomotives.

11. TECHNOLOGY. Commisioning of new Oxted signalbox, first solid state electronic box on Southern Region.

15. NEW LINE. Plans announced for new nine-mile 15 in. gauge line on Great Eastern freight line from Wroxham, lifted 1982.

16. ELECTRIFICATION. £675,000 scheme for 6½ mile Watford–St. Albans Abbey line announced.

16. PRESERVATION. Steam returns to Cambrian Line with use of GWR-design Manor Class 2–6–0 7819 HINTON MANOR *on Machynlleth–Aberystwyth excursion*.

16. RESTORATION. 30th birthday of Hastings gauge DEMUs marked by outshopping of four-car Class 203 unit 203 001 unit in green livery.

17. CLOSURE. Welshpool freight yard.

18. LOCOMOTIVES. First Class 09 withdrawn from capital stock – 09017 sent to Sudbrook for Severn Tunnel Junction emergency train.

18 and 19. OPEN DAYS. Planned festival of Transport at CEGB Trawsfynydd abandoned.

19. PRESERVATION. Return to steam after restoration at Birmingham Railway Museum of GWR Castle Class 4–6–0 5080 *DEFIANT*.

20. LOCOMOTIVES. Withdrawal of second Class 50 loco 50006 *Neptune* at Laira. Despatched to Crewe for spares recovery.

21. RAILFREIGHT. New Westbury–Harlow stone trains bring

10. PRESERVATION. Classes 27, 40, 55 and EM2 break new ground with use on Severn Valley Railway.

10. PRESERVATION. Return to traffic after restoration of ex-Barry loco BR Class 4 2–6–4T 80080 at Midland Railway Trust, Butterley.

11. NEW REGION. Marylebone and Chiltern Line services handed over to Western Region control. New LMR boundary is Fenny Compton.

12. CLOSURE. Severn Tunnel Junction depot, work transferred to Newport East Usk yard and Cardiff Tidal Sidings. 233 staff dispersed.

12. RENOVATION. Work starts on 18-month, £3.6 million, conversion of Ilkley station into shops complex.

12. LOCOMOTIVES. Class 91 bodyshell moved from BREL Crewe to Wimpey Laboratories at Hayes, Middlesex for drawbar loads tests.

15. RAILFREIGHT. New BR locomotive freight liveries unveiled at Ripple Lane open day. Public open day follows on 17th.

16. MISHAPS. Severe 100 mph storms devastate South East and 5000 fallen trees plus debris close most BR routes for several days. Dover Western Docks train ferry pier sustains £300,000 damage

17. PRESERVATION. Steam returns to West Highland Line with LMS Class 5 4–6–0 No 5305 over 100 miles from Fort William to Craigendoran.

17. PRESERVATION. Deltic Preservation Society celebrates 10th anniversary by using 55015 *TULYAR* and 55019 *ROYAL HIGHLAND FUSILIER* on services at Midland Railway Trust.

17. CEREMONY. Class 33 loco No 33112 named *Templecombe* after re-opened LSWR station, 112 miles from Waterloo.

18. MISHAP. GWR Totnes station bridge destroyed by BR civil engineer's raised crane jib.

19. MISHAP. Glanrhyd tragedy. Three passengers and driver of two-car 05.28 Shrewsbury–Swansea DMU die when it plunges into flooded river owing to the collapse of 127-year-old Towy bridge.

19. RETIREMENT. ASLEF General Secretary Ray Buckton, aged 65.

19. IRELAND. Irish Rail leases three 80 Class DEMUs from NIR for non-electrified services in Dublin area.

20 NEW SERVICE. Ribble Rail Day marked by four specials on Preston–Clitheroe freight route.

22. TECHNOLOGY. Tredegar firm Hugh Phillips Engineering compltes three scratch-built personnel carriers for Sudan Railways hopes for orders

from British preserved lines.

23. IRELAND. NIR Newry and Portadown services dislocated by heavy flooding and landslips.

23. LOCOMOTIVES. Five withdrawn Class 45 Peaks re-instated as 97409–13 for East Coast Main Line electrification work.

24. PRESERVATION. Diesel and Electric Group disel open day at GWS depot, Didcot, includes Foster Yeoman Class 59.

27. PRESERVATION. Return to UK after 47 years in France, and Dunkerque battles, of LMS 350 hp shunter 7069, delivered to Swanage Railway.

29. RAILFREIGHT. Princess Anne opens Amey Roadstone's £25 million facelifted Whatley quarry , Somerset, and names Railfreight Class 56 loco 56001 *Whatley*.

31. LOCOMOTIVES. First Class 90 electric 90001 outshopped from Crewe Works. To Derby RTC for tests.

31. CLOSURE. Old Margan Hump Yard.

NOVEMBER

1. SPEED RECORD. HST power cars 43102 and 43159 beat the world diesel traction record with 148.5 mph south of Northallerton on ECML.

1. RAILFREIGHT. New Margan Knuckle Yard opened to replace old hump complex.

2. RENOVATION. Long-delayed £3 million clean-up for 147-year-old Stockport Viaduct gets under way with 70 jobs created.

3. TECHNOLOGY. Director of Civil Engineering receives new track recording unit, Class 150/1 Sprinter bodied DB 999600/1, at Paddington ceremony.

6. NEW STATION. Waungron Park, Cardiff.

7. LOCOMOTIVES. Bids close for 100 new BR Class 60s. Only three of six invited firms decide to tender namely Metro-Cammell, Brush Electrical Machines, and GEC Transportation Projects.

10. NEW STOCK. First Metro-Cammell Class 156 Sprinter DMU delivered to BR from Washwood Heath works.

11. RAILFREIGHT Speedlink VIP special brings first electric-hauled train to Peterborough with LM loco 85011.

13. RENOVATION. New parkway scheme and 250-space car park opened at Newton Abbot.

13. PRESERVATION. Redundant Stamford Midland Railway signalbox moved 400 yards to new home at station, occupied by bookseller

Robert Humm.

16. LOCOMOTIVES New Class 90 Electric 90001 towed from Derby RTC to Melton Mowbray for trials

17. NEW STOCK. BR orders 194 Class 158 Super Sprinter 23-metre DMU vehicles for Provincial Services at cost of £69 million. Routes earmarked are North Trans-Pennine Cardiff–Southampton, East Anglia–North-West/Birmingham, and Glasgow–Aberdeen. Option on 10 more vehicles.

19. TECHNOLOGY. New Euston £500,000 passenger information board commissioned, purportedly the world's largest liquid crystal display.

19. PRIVATISATION. BR revises terms of Vale of Rheidol narrow gauge sell-off – scrap dealers are not eligible, only firms to keep it a going concern.

20. PRESERVATION. Stars Michael Caine and Ben Kingsley at Lakeside and Haverthwaite Railway's Lakeside station to film ""The Imposter of Baker Street".

23. TECHNOLOGY. Work starts on 19-week scheme to eradicate landslip problems on half-mile of Wickford–Rayleigh line.

24. WORKS. BREL Crewe, York Derby Loco and Derby Carriage Works offered for sale as one concern under government privatisation scheme. Horwich Foundry to be sold separately.

25. MISHAP. Class 37 locos 37670/1 seriously damaged in derailment with tankers in Tavistock Junction yard, Plymouth.

26. PRESERVATION. Ceremony at Marylebone marks 50th anniversary of naming by its designer of LNER A4 4–6–2 4498 *SIR NIGEL GRESLEY*.

29. CUTBACK. Massive track cutbacks at March Whitemoor yard.

30. NEW SERVICE. Amended timetable eases service problems and punctuality on Cardiff Valley Lines.

30. POLICY CHANGE. Durham open station scheme abandoned to curb fare evasion on short journeys from Darlington and Newcastle.

30. TRANSFERRED. Final disgraced Cornish Class 142 Skipper units moved to Newton Heath.

30. SCRAPPED. At Mayer Newman, Newmarket, prototype refurbished DMUs, Metro-Cammell Class 101 vehicles 51451 and 51518.

DECEMBER

4. UNIONS. NUR General Secretary Jimmy Knapp visits South Wales amd backs call for more Sprinter DMUs to ease overcrowding, and deplores fare increases 50 per cent above ination.

LOCOMOTIVES. Withdrawal at aira of third Class 50, 50014 *Wars-ite.*

and 6. TECHNOLOGY. Final ages of Leicester area resignalling heme completed.

MISHAP. Thirsk ticket and par-els offices, due for modernisation, estroyed by fire.

TECHNOLOGY. Radio Electro-ic Token Block (RETB) system ommissioned on 42-mile Fort Wil-am and Mallaig route, delayed be-ause of interference of emergency ervices wavelengths and TV in Eire.

MISHAP. Four PW men killed ter beng struck by DMU at Meth-y Junction, Wakefield.

FOR SALE. Trackbed of March–palding line closed 1982 offered to ndowners.

0. WORKS. Tarmac unveils plans r £250 million redevelopment of osed BREL Swindon site with ops, factories and homes. " A" op to be demolished during 1988.

0. ROYAL VISIT. The Queen isits Bulmers factory at Hereford nd sees two locos in steam, LMS rincess Royal Class 4–6–2 6201 *RINCESS ELIZABETH,* and WR King Class 4–6–0 6000 *KING EORGE V.*

10. LOCOMOTIVES. Withdrawal of BR's last Class 24, Derby RTC 97201 *Experiment*, displaced by Class 31.

11. CRIME. Police investigate theft of £12.5 million from BR headquarters.

11. SPECIAL WORKING. EMU shortage on GN suburban line sees LMR electric loco 86403 used with West Highland green and cream Mark 1 stock on 16.35 Kings Cross–Peterborough commuter service.

11. PRESERVATION. Ex-Barry GWR-design Manor Class 2–6–0 7828 raises steam for first time since rebuilding at Toddington, Gloucestershire and Warwickshire Railway.

13. CLOSURE. Woodhead tracklifting trains less than a mile from Hadfield, Manchester at western end.

14. NEW SERVICE.First revenue-earning push-pull train on WCML with modified HST power car 43123, 0926 Wolverhampton–Euston, with 86240 as powered loco.

14. PRESERVATION. Another ex-Barry restoration – LMS 3F 0–6–0T 47279 steam-tested on Keighley and Worth Valley Railway.

15. MISHAP. Four seriously injured as Class 150 Sprinter DMU 150 212 on the 0628 Scarborough–York collides with unmanned crane parked on same track.

18. NEW STOCK. First unit of new Bournemouth line Class 442 EMU stock handed over to NSE at BREL Derby Carriage Works.

18. RENOVATION. Ceremony marks completion of Motherwell station modernisation.

18. RENOVATION. Highland Regional Council-sponsored restoration of Scottish ski capital Aviemore station finished.

21. CRIME. Leeds station cleared and trains halted as police chase armed gunman. No injuries, man escapes.

30. PRESERVATION. Scottish Railway Preservation Society starts 11-day movement of stock from Falkirk to Bo'ness after 20 years to make way for redevelopment.

31. LOCOMOTIVES. March depot loses allocation, Class 31/4s to Bescot, Class 08 shunters to Cambridge.

31. PRESERVATION. 100th birthday of Barton Wright L&Y 0–6–0 52044 on Keighley and Worth Valley Railway.

31. PRESERVATION. Three steam locomotives remain unsold at Barry scrapyard, GWR 2–8–0s 2873 and 3845, and BR Class 4 2–6–4T 80072.

31. LOCOMOTIVES. BR outlines plans for dual-voltage Class 92 freight loco for Channel Tunnel traffic.

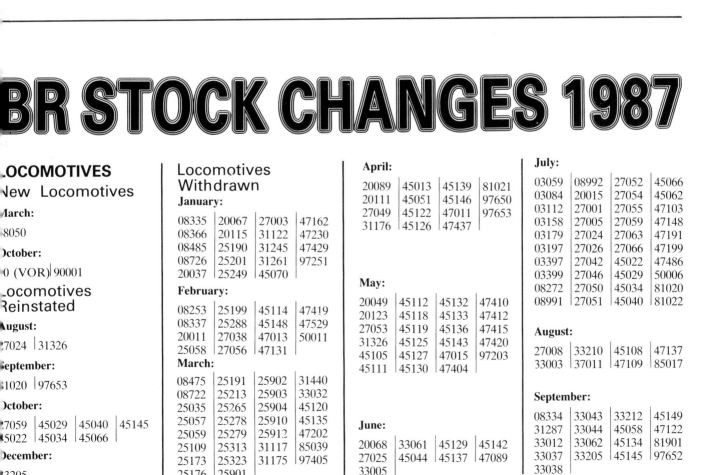

BR STOCK CHANGES 1987

LOCOMOTIVES

New Locomotives

March:
8050

October:
0 (VOR) | 90001

Locomotives Reinstated

August:
27024 | 31326

September:
1020 | 97653

October:

27059	45029	45040	45145
5022	45034	45066	

December:
3205

Locomotives Withdrawn

January:

08335	20067	27003	47162
08366	20115	31122	47230
08485	25190	31245	47429
08726	25201	31261	97251
20037	25249	45070	

February:

08253	25199	45114	47419
08337	25288	45148	47529
20011	27038	47013	50011
25058	27056	47131	

March:

08475	25191	25902	31440
08722	25213	25903	33032
25035	25265	25904	45120
25057	25278	25910	45135
25059	25279	25912	47202
25109	25313	31117	85039
25173	25323	31175	97405
25176	25901		

April:

20089	45013	45139	81021
20111	45051	45146	97650
27049	45122	47011	97653
31176	45126	47437	

May:

20049	45112	45132	47410
20123	45118	45133	47412
27053	45119	45136	47415
31326	45125	45143	47420
45105	45127	47015	97203
45111	45130	47404	

June:

20068	33061	45129	45142
27025	45044	45137	47089
33005			

July:

03059	08992	27052	45066
03084	20015	27054	45062
03112	27001	27055	47103
03158	27005	27059	47148
03179	27024	27063	47191
03197	27026	27066	47199
03397	27042	45022	47486
03399	27046	45029	50006
08272	27050	45034	81020
08991	27051	45040	81022

August:

27008	33210	45108	47137
33003	37011	47109	85017

September:

08334	33043	33212	45149
31287	33044	45058	47122
33012	33062	45134	81901
33037	33205	45145	97652
33038			

October:

08728	27059	33105	82005
08736	33045	45049	97250

November:

03063	20150	20167	20220
03089	20153	20181	20221
03371	20155	20191	20223
08394	20162	20216	45121
20149	20164		

December:

08400	45144	82008	97201
20222	50014		

Locomotives Renumbered

From	To	From	To
08462	08994	37135	37888
08687	08995	37149	37892
09017	98706	37164	37675
20304	20168	37166	37891
31326	97204	37168	37890
37001	37707	37169	37674
37014	37709	37182	37670
37016	37706	37189	37672
37018	37517	37224	37680
37027	37519	37233	37689
37041	37520	37237	37893
37060	37705	37247	37671
37076	37518	37256	37678
37086	37516	45022	97409
37089	37708	45029	97410
37120	37887	45034	97411
37121	37677	45040	97412
37123	37679	45066	97413
37126	37676	47232	47665
37129	37669	50049	50149
37130	37681	81021	81901
37133	37673	86007	86407

Locomotives Transferred to Static Departmental Use and Renumbered

January:

25908	ADB 968026
25912	ADB 968027
27204	ADB 968028

COACHING STOCK
New Coaches
Undated:

2922 2923

Coaches Withdrawn
Undated:

4331	4508	4666	34666
4345	4575	4672	35128
4406	4593		

January:

5169	7944	18379	24888
5190	11025	18592	24890
5923	11061	24844	24894
5990	12074	24848	24900
6169	13480	24856	35069
7161	18365	24880	35070
7174	18369	24884	35114
7204			

February:

3092	5134	7181	18828

3094	5297	13420	24841
4799	6407	18286	24857
5120	7120	18401	34528

March:

3122	5328	18289	18975
3600	5348	18309	34525
3727	5407	18361	34675
3730	9411	18739	35124
5242	13085	18777	35125
5250	13333	18874	35182
5313	17026	18905	

April:

3085	7650	18422	35131
7157	13413	18801	35477
7630	17045	35054	

May:

4354	7201	9011	18787
5390	9000	9014	19476
5507	9003	18381	35043
7200			

June:

3214	7198	9395	18720
5332	7223	13234	34667
5411	7230	18408	35065
5428	7919	18563	35071
6426	7930	18707	35126
7076	9387		

July:

1712	7926	13449	18860
5074	7942	13530	18862
5075	7943	17029	18878
5092	7950	18403	18891
5100	7973	18416	18965
5106	9403	18565	19020
5108	13384	18574	19504
5123	13389	18575	21275
5319	13392	18576	34524
5344	13394	18587	34555
6410	13395	18607	35010
6441	13398	18754	35048
7113	13399	18804	35051
7155	13400	18808	35058
7191	13401	18811	35115
7197	13403	18837	35177
7644	13404	18846	35186
7663	13416	18854	35189
7673	13424	18855	35461
7918	13439		

August:

3072	4476	7924	34661
4372	5185	18362	35057
4474	5229	19481	

September:

1748	3843	7185	18764
1874	3845	7211	19457
3738	3846	7215	19466
3745	3848	7217	19501
3746	4033	7218	19505
3748	4035	13332	19511
3759	4055	18615	19557
3828	4074	18670	24834
3837	4371	18671	35176
3838	5562	18761	

October:

1555	4755	5389	19484
1701	5084	13487	34676
4031	5218	18988	34680
4389	5324		

November:

1814	4306	4775	5091
3607	4494	5048	5093
4050	4561	5049	5096
4094	4571	5053	13524
4211	4579	5055	18301
4243	4610	5057	18330
4258	4623	5060	18383
4279	4643	5067	18753
4303	4706		

December:

6409	18377	18845	34521
7224	18770	19019	34523
13415	18779	19485	34530
13421	18832	19491	34551
13528	18839	19515	34560
13531	18843	19518	34672
13554			

Coaches Reinstated
December:

5389

Coaches Renumbered

From	To	From	To
3602	3144	11041	10216
3604	3147	11043	10223
3308	6703	11047	10219
3346	6701	11049	10212
3347	6700	11050	10213
3380	6464	11051	10217
3422	6465	11053	10218
10001	10260	11056	10220
10002	10242	11057	10227
10003	10240	11059	10229
10004	10234	11062	10224
10005	10248	11063	10222
10006	10254	19479	13479
10007	10257	19488	19488
10008	10252	19513	13513
10009	10241	35197	80218
10010	10255	35201	80219
10011	10247	35276	80220
10012	10249	35279	80209
10013	10233	35282	80210
10014	10246	35292	80215
10015	10235	35296	80211
10016	10231	35299	80217
10017	10238	35304	80206
10018	10236	35307	80212
10019	10245	35315	80222
10020	10250	35316	80213
10021	10230	35323	80214
10022	10237	35341	80208
10023	10258	35466	80207
10024	10251	40502	10204
10025	10259	40503	10205
10026	10253	40504	10202
10027	10232	40506	10203
10028	10256	40507	10206
11012	10221	40508	10209
11014	10225	40509	10210
11015	10226	40510	10211
11032	10215	40516	10207
11034	10214	40517	10208
11035	10228		

Coaches on Hire to DSB

From	To DSB		
10664	50 86 75-72	064-5	
10667	50 86 75-72	067-8	
10668	50 86 75-72	068-6	
10669	50 86 75-72	069-4	
10676	50 86 75-72	076-9	
10677	50 86 75-72	077-7	
10694	50 86 75-72	094-2	
10695	50 86 75-72	095-9	
10698	50 86 75-72	098-3	
10721	50 86 75-72	021-5	

DIESEL MULTIPLE UNITS
New DMUs

January:

142 064	150 218	150 221
142 066	150 219	150 222
144 008	150 220	150 223

February:

142 067	144 010	150 228
142 068	144 012	150 230
142 069	150 204	150 231
142 070	150 224	150 233
142 076	150 225	150 234
142 079	150 226	150 236
144 009		

March:

142 049	144 014	150 227
142 077	144 015	150 229
142 080	144 016	150 232
142 081	150 203	150 235
142 082	150 205	150 237
142 084	150 206	150 238
142 085	150 207	150 239
142 089	150 208	150 240
142 090	150 209	150 241
142 091	150 210	150 242
144 013	150 211	150 243

April:

142 087	150 212	150 248
142 088	150 213	150 249
142 092	150 244	150 250
144 017	150 245	150 251
144 018	150 246	150 252
144 020	150 247	150 255
150 201		

May:

142 075	150 214	150 258
142 086	150 216	150 259
142 093	150 253	150 260
142 094	150 254	150 261
144 019	150 256	150 262
144 021	150 257	155 301

June:

142 095	150 264	150 268
144 022	150 265	150 269
150 215	150 266	150 270
150 217	150 267	150 271
150 263		

July:

142 083	150 272	150 276
142 096	150 273	150 277
144 023	150 274	

August:

150 275	150 279	155 302
150 278		

September:

150 280	150 282	155 303
150 281		

October:

50 283	155 304	155 306
50 284	155 305	

November:

55 307	155 309	156 401
55 308		

December:

55 310	155 312	155 313
55 311		

DMUs Withdrawn

Undated:

51233	51536	53175	59067
51239	53138	53184	59071
51240	53143	53748	59088
51242	53147	59047	59269
51251	53174		

January:

51294	52078	78707	78957
51581	53140	78710	78973
51585	53199	78724	78974
51810			

February:

51096	52068	54066	54394
51105	53136	54076	59356
51590	53167	54190	59420
51844	53603	54344	59474

March:

51176	51782	53648	59066
51186	51788	53652	59268
51193	51790	53698	59285
51198	51814	53737	59326
51235	51815	53738	59342
51237	51820	53821	59371
51293	51825	53840	59440
51469	51841	53860	59441
51478	51846	53868	59557
51502	52079	53882	59559
51573	52083	53892	59567
51576	53068	53918	59580
51578	53104	54198	59623
51582	53105	54199	59681
51587	53148	54336	59682
51781	53210	54411	

April:

53057	53130	53725	54119
53064	53704	53729	59476
53088	53714	53831	

May:

51284	53226	54021	54133
51299	53375	54025	54143
51574	53381	54026	54182
51580	53852	54032	54183
53069	54003	54035	54195
53099	54016	54045	54420
53111	54017	54115	59548

June:

51077	54051	54092	54373
53453	54053	54192	54376
53623	54058	54193	54383
53845	54059	54199	54390
53883	54064	54339	54392
53898	54067	54366	54409
53903	54082	54371	59362
53912	54088		

July:

51819	53144	54359	59545
51822	53172	59053	59566
51831	53254	59369	59569
51832	53861	59413	78716
51833	53864	59431	78966
53098	53917	59436	

August:

51068	51783	53362	59429
51072	51787	53672	59480
51085	51816	53708	78708
51098	53074	53739	78721
51200	53094	53828	78723
51311	53304	53915	78958
51326	53328	59297	78963
51575	53329	59357	78972

September:

51067	53134	53259	59415
51786	53135	53295	59730
51084	53137	53320	

October:

51069	51466	53875	59037
51075	51518	53985	59038
51092	51535	54063	59041
51097	51785	54349	59065
51098	51805	59030	59355
51451	51807	59033	59363
51452	53067	59034	59470
51452	53153	59035	59472
51453	53456	59036	59557
51459	53514		

November:

51236	53062	53127	59281
51470	53076	53179	59297
51528	53097	53183	59428
51534	53103	53192	59533
51539	53110	53885	59691
51797	53118	59097	

December:

51313	53434	53905	59434
51328	53819	53906	59438
51910	53823	59329	59439
51934	53824	59354	59443
52037	53835	59423	59634
53075	53846	59426	59640
53108	53876	59432	59647
53424	53896		

DMUs Reinstated

Undated:

53456	54033	53514

March:

59104	59124

April:

54199	54392

June:

51587	54034	54356

July:

59557

August:

54371

November:

59415

DMUs Renumbered

From	To	From	To
53362	55945	54356	6300
54034	55933		

DEMUs Withdrawn

Undated:

60803, 77503/8 (204).
60108/20, 60657/8, 60808/20 (205).

August:

60100, 60807, 77500 (204)

September:

60104/18, 60653/54, 60804/18 (205).

October:

60022/45 (202).
60102, 60802, 77507 (204).
60105/9/16/19, 60652/5/6/9/66, 60805/6/9/16/19 (205).
60044, 60561, 60812 (206).
60128/31/32/36/37/39/40/41/43, 60602/5/6/8/10/11/13/14/15/17, 60902/5/6/8/10/11/13/14/15/17 (207).

ELECTRIC MULTIPLE UNITS

New EMUs

March:

317 370	317 371

August:

317 372

September:

319 001	319 002

October:

319 003	319 004

November:

319 005	319 007	319 009
319 006	319 008	319 010

Vehicles Withdrawn

Undated:

65360, 77106/11/545 (416).
76108 (421).
70893 (423).

February:

61126/97/204, 70126/97, 75240/54/61/316 (302).

March:

65392/435, 77110/2 (416).

May:

65435, 77578 (416).

June:

61643, 75675/95 (304).

July:

75626 (303).
62177, 76417/36 (311).
14011/33/34/47/48/49/55/67/68/100/215/16/17/18/43/44/69/84/327/28/37/71/72/73/84/584 (415).
15006/14/17/24/25/102/6/17/24/25/34/41/62/71/73/83/86/87/90/203/70/92/314/28/42/70 (415).
65311/12/13/14/15/16/91, 77100/1/2/3/4/5/9 (416).
22, 41/2/6 (485).

September:

14219/349/60, 15043/131/238/358, 61625/6 (415).

November:

76404/23, 62164 (311).

NPCCS Withdrawn

January:

84070	84438	93517

February:

84116	84349	93373	93964
84128	84576	93814	

March:

80552	80815	93488	93877
80625	80975	93594	93921
80751	84148	93676	94885
80765	93274		

April:

99600

May:

80811	94595	94677	94708
94283	94673	94688	94834

June:

80661	84583	93358	94564
80866	93183	94014	94880

July:

84611	96290	96291	96295
93146			

August:

99608

November:

84407

December:

80527

NPCCS Reinstated

October:

93094	93945

November:

93928

December:

93599

NPCCS Renumbered

From	To	From	To
80461	84387	93344	96157
80462	84461	93355	96159
80463	84477	93440	96173
80560	95207	93443	96161
80614	95303	93448	96190
80689	95300	93641	96176
80863	95305	93691	96134
84060	84382	93738	96110
84124	95307	93742	96111
84161	95308	93743	96102
84292	95310	93744	96103
84345	95304	93748	96137
93083	96185	93749	96138
93087	96186	93750	96112
93097	96150	93751	96139
93324	96152	93752	96140
93326	96171	93755	96135
93331	96154	93447	96189

BR NAMINGS & DENAMINGS

LOCOMOTIVES NAMED DURING 1987

FEBRUARY

03	37905	Vulcan Enterprise	Cardiff Canton TMD
21	37501	Teesside Steelmaster	Thornaby TMD
	47564	COLOSSUS	Cardiff Canton TMD
	47576	Kings Lynn	Kings Lynn

MARCH

02	47291	Port of Felixtowe	Felixtowe Docks
10	37412	Loch Lomond	Eastfield TMD
14	58049	Littleton Colliery	Littleton Colliery
	37413	Loch Eil Outward Bound	Eastfield TMD
	37502	British Steel Teesside	Thornaby TMD
	37504	British Steel Corby	Thornaby TMD
	37506	British Steel Skinningrove	Thornaby TMD

APRIL

07	47635	Jimmy Milne	Glasgow Central
28	47350	British Petroleum	Thame
28	47563	Woman's Guild	Edinburgh Waverley
29	87006	Glasgow Garden Festival	Glasgow Central
	37429	Sir Dyfed/County of Dyfed	Cardiff Canton TMD
	37505	British Steel Workington	Thornaby TMD

MAY

01	43019	Dinas Abertawe/ City of Swansea	Swansea
01	47411	The Geordie	Gateshead TMD
06	43017	HTV West	Bristol Temple Meads
08	73118	The Romney, Hythe and Dymchurch Railway	Folkestone Harbour
09	58050	Toton Traction Depot	Toton TMD
11	43151	Blue Peter II	Newcastle
11	47622	The Institution of Mechanical Engineers	Bristol Temple Meads
11	86220	The Round Tabler	Norwich
11	86221	BBC Look East	London Liverpool Street
13	37513	Thornaby Demon	Thornaby TMD
14	31309	Cricklewood	Cricklewood TMD
14	47016	Toleman Group	Dagenham
16	37428	David Lloyd George	Pwhelli
27	31327	Phillips - Imperial	ICI Teesside
28	37411	The Institution of Railway Signal Engineers	Oban
30	08869	The Canary	Norwich Crown Point TMD
31	47348	St Christopher's Railway Home	Coalville Sidings

JUNE

01	73124	London Chamber of Commerce	London Cannon Street
04	20122	Cleveland Potash	Boulby
04	20137	Murray B Hofmeyr	Boulby
16	47637	Springburn	Springburn BRML
17	37431	Sir Powys/County of Powys	Llandrindod Wells
17	86222	LLOYDS LIST 250th ANNIVERSARY	Colchester
20	51899	Aylesbury College SILVER JUBILEE 1987	Aylesbury
23	86430	Scottish National Orchestra	Glasgow Central
	50040	Centurion	Laira TMD

JULY

03	73117	University of Surrey	London Waterloo
04	43051	The Duke and Duchess of York	York
16	86407	The Institution of Electrical Engineers	Crewe ETD
22	37671	Tre Pol and Pen	Laira TMD
24	37503	British Steel Shelton	Thornaby TMD

AUGUST

04	37429	Eisteddfod Genedlaethol	Porthmadog
10	86432	Brookside	Liverpool Lime Street
13	20118	Saltburn by the Sea	Saltburn
13	20165	Henry Pease	Saltburn
20	56131	Ellington Colliery	Ellington Colliery
	37675	William Cookworthy	Laira TMD
	47574	Benjamin Gimbert G.C.	Stratford TMD

SEPTEMBER

12	60014	St Leonards	St Leonards depot
14	37672	Freight Transport Association	Stratford upon Avon
19	73004	The Bluebell Railway	East Grinstead
20	47214	Tinsley Traction Depot	Tinsley TMD
23	37068	Grainflow	Ely
25	47380	Immingham	Immingham Docks

OCTOBER

03	47142	The Sapper	Long Marston MOD
03	47522	Doncaster Enterprise	Doncaster Major Depot
06	43132	Worshipful Company of Carmen	London Paddington
17	37892	Ripple Lane	Ripple Lane
20	56001	Whatley	Whatley Quarry
22	47501	Craftsman	London Paddington
29	56095	Harworth Colliery	Harworth Colliery
31	33112	Templecombe	Templecombe
	08995	KIDWELLY	Landore TMD

NOVEMBER

03	37325	Coal Merchant's Association of Scotland	Aberdeen
04	73105	Quadrant	London Victoria
04	86408	St John Ambulance	London Euston
07	37799	Sir Dyfed County of Dyfed	Cardiff Canton TMD

DECEMBER

01	47207	Bulmers of Hereford	Hereford
01	86223	Norwich Union	Norwich
04	37507	Hartlepool Pipe Mill	Hartlepool
09	37424	Glendarroch	Glasgow Queen Street

LOCOMOTIVE NAMES REMOVED DURING 1987

FEBRUARY

37027	Loch Eil
37062	British Steel Corby
37078	Teesside Steelmaster

MARCH

37071	British Steel Skinningrove
37095	British Steel Teesside
37180	Sir Dyfed/County of Dyfed

APRIL

37066	British Steel Workington
47633	ORION
87006	City of Glasgow

MAY

47574	LLOYDS LIST 250th ANNIVERSARY
47577	Benjamin Gimbert G.C.
86220	Goliath
86221	Vesta
86223	Hector

JUNE

50040	Leviathan
86222	Fury

JULY

37077	British Steel Shelton
37196	Tre Pol and Pen
37207	William Cookworthy

AUGUST

37429	Sir Dyfed/County of Dyfed

SEPTEMBER

47079	G J CHURCHWARD

OCTOBER

47120	RAF Kinloss